In Memory and Appreciation of Frances S. Hatfield

School Library
Media Programs:
Focus on
Trends and Issues
No. 11

DESIGNING AND RENOVATING SCHOOL LIBRARY MEDIA CENTERS

Jane P. Klasing

American Library Association
Chicago and London 1991

Jane P. Klasing is the director of Learning Resources for the school board of Broward County in Florida where she is responsible for providing leadership, program development and basic media services to the total school program. She is editor of *Florida Media Quarterly* and consulting editor to *School Library Media Quarterly*. She has published several articles in professional journals such as *School Library Journal* and *Wisconsin Library Journal* and is active in numerous professional associations.

Text and cover design by Gordon Stromberg

Composed in Garth Graphic by WordWorks, Davenport, Iowa, on a Xyvision/Compugraphic 8600

Printed on 50-pound Glatfelter, a pH-neutral stock, and bound in 10-point C1S cover stock by McNaughton & Gunn

The paper used in this publication meets the minimum requirements of American National Standard for Information Sciences—Permanence of Paper for Printed Library Materials, ANSI Z39.48–1984. ∞

Library of Congress Cataloging-in-Publication Data

Klasing, Jane P.
    Designing and renovating school library media centers
/ by Jane P. Klasing.
        p. cm. — (School library media programs ; no. 11)
    Includes bibliographical references and index.
    ISBN 0-8389-0560-9
    1. Library architecture. 2. Library buildings.
3. School libraries. 4. Media programs (Education)
I. Title. II. Series.
Z679.K53   1991   90-27857
027.8—dc20   CIP

Printed in the United States of America.

95   5 4 3

CONTENTS

FIGURES

EDITOR'S INTRODUCTION

This volume is a response to an important and immediate professional need. Knowledge of facilities planning has not traditionally been a priority in the education of school library media specialists. In the past, practitioners had relatively little direct influence on such planning, and economic constraints further limited opportunities for participation. That situation has changed, however. Currently there is a great deal of building and remodeling activity in school systems nationwide, as well as increasing awareness that library media center facilities design involves special considerations related to new information technologies. School library media professionals are being presented with opportunities to participate in the facilities planning process; simultaneously they are being challenged by the need to better understand this process.

Any professional who has lived through a building project, whether at home or in the workplace, knows that the usual operating mode is survival. There are many interdependent groups involved in implementing such a project; communication can be a challenge even in the best of situations. Too often, problems are unanticipated and important information either is not given or is misunderstood. Those who ultimately will be using the space generally feel frustrated, impotent, and, in the worst situations, angry and demoralized.

Designing and Renovating School Library Media Centers is based on Jane Klasing's experiences as the director of learning resources in a large school district implementing a major long-range program for facilities expansion and renewal. Working with district administrators, school board members, architects, building-level administrators, teachers, and library media specialists, Klasing developed a practical model for facilitating effective planning and communication among these constituencies. She has used this model in guiding and successfully completing 58 projects involving new construction or renovation of a school library media center.

The book is specifically intended to help practitioners systematically articulate program needs in a style and language that architects, engineers, and builders can understand and, at the same time, to demystify the arcane language of specialists responsible for design and construction. This is a propitious moment for library media specialists to take advantage of the momentum provided by such innovations in school culture as site-based management, and by the existence of aging buildings to interpret and highlight the library media program as part of the facilities planning process. This volume, in part the result of a practitioner-architect partnership, will provide many of the tools needed to forge the powerful partnerships advocated in *Information Power.*

ELEANOR R. KULLESEID
Series Editor

ACKNOWLEDGMENTS

It is frequently lamented that practitioners—those out in the trenches—fail to share their experiences with their colleagues through the professional literature. Without the support and encouragement of those who have mentored; those, including my husband, who shared technical expertise over the years of my involvement in school building construction projects; and the committed staff of administrators, support personnel, and school library media specialists with whom I work, my own contribution would be among the unshared.

Beginning in the early sixties with my first involvement in school library media center construction, there was the mentoring of my advisor, Frances Henne. Later, the administration of school library media programs under the tutelage of Frances Hatfield, strong professional associations with my colleagues, and the patient mentoring which sometimes, of necessity, became prodding from Shirley Aaron and Eleanor Kulleseid, provided the inspiration for this project.

Special gratitude goes to Katherine Butera-Palmer who never hesitated when the many changes in the narrative were necessary, and who has untiringly supported the school library media profession. For those architects and project managers who had to participate in the "dialogue," appreciation cannot be measured. Special thanks to Gary Kuhl, principal with Scharf and Associates, Fort Lauderdale, Florida; to Pam Spencer and Nancy Bard of Fairfax County School District, Virginia, for their major contribution to this book; to Luther Eubanks of Frimet Design, Hollywood, Florida, for his creative contribution in writing a portion of the book, developing illustrations, and participating with me in speaking engagements; and to Eleanor Kulleseid who edited and worked as hard as I on this project. My appreciation for the contribution of all who participated, and to family and friends who waited patiently, is unmeasurable.

INTRODUCTION

The Background

A fledgling school library media professional in the early sixties, I was privileged to hear Ruth Weinstock address school administrators just before the release of the Educational Facilities Laboratory's landmark report on *The School Library: Facilities for Independent Study in the Secondary School.*[1] Weinstock urged the audience to consider the importance of individual inquiry and the implications of planning learning environments that encourage the independent pursuit of knowledge. She suggested that libraries should integrate the newer communications media with the old, print-based methods. She reminded listeners that new and remodeled school facilities would need the flexibility to respond to rapid and pervasive changes in information technology. The administrators' reaction to these concepts was one of vocal disbelief. Although the facilities described and recommended by the Educational Facilities Laboratory in 1963 were feasible, educators and the general public were not ready. They had no "technological" mind-set.

The concepts presented by Weinstock are still valid, but contemporary planners of school library facilities are facing the consequences of decisions, or lack of them, made a generation ago. Many of the decision makers chose to ignore the need for flexibility and newer communications delivery systems for school library media centers. These centers were a vital part of the boom in school building construction in the 1960s and 1970s; today they contribute to the aging building syndrome that faces school districts nationwide.

The problem has been exacerbated by a number of changes. Among the most visible are rapid advances in technology and in the systems for delivering information—advances anticipated nearly thirty years ago by the Educational Facilities Laboratory. In addition, an expanding knowledge base has made a significant impact on curriculum development and the delivery of instruction as well as on the size of library media collections. Another important change is the trend toward expanded use of the school library media center when school is not in session. Last, but not least, are changes in population size and composition; some school districts are dealing with significant reductions in student numbers while others are facing growth in birth rates or a great influx of new populations. Students arrive at school with different learning styles and needs—some, the results of societal changes and widespread substance abuse, completely new to our experience.

Older buildings are simply unable to meet current challenges for delivery of both programs and information. Educational planners are now forced to assess needs and to consider the possibility that the existing facilities compromise the quality of educational opportunities within a school or district. Planning done in the sixties and seventies rarely resulted in facilities that can accommodate the changes needed to meet today's educational challenges.

With a greater emphasis on the need to accommodate newer technologies and delivery systems, planners today must allow the need for built-in flexibility in spaces to dominate the process. Private sector corporations are planning office environments with an eye to the future, providing parallels and the rationale for educators who must consider new, renovated, or expanded school library media centers. Planning for present needs cannot be the engine that drives the process. Planning for flexible space and future needs will enable reconfiguration of library media centers as collections grow and change in emphases; as programs, teaching, and learning styles change; and even as newer technologies emerge.

The Purpose of This Book

School library media specialists are seldom prepared by training or experience to meet the challenges of planning for new or renovated facilities. This publication is intended to help fill gaps both in the practitioner's knowledge base and in a professional literature that has given limited attention to school library media facilities planning in the past two decades. *Media Center Facilities Design* is the major facilities document of the seventies, and one of the best of a small number of titles.[2] The perception that little recent research or scholarship has been devoted to this topic is reinforced by E. Blanche Woolls and by the chapter on facilities in the latest edition of professional standards, *Information Power: Guidelines for School Library Media Programs*.[3] Architectural issues of professional journals deal predominantly with academic and public library buildings,[4] yet this emphasis does not reflect actual construction activity. In 1987 alone, public library projects were completed at a cost of $217 million, while school building construction projects were completed to the tune of $9.2 billion.[5] Figure 1 shows the

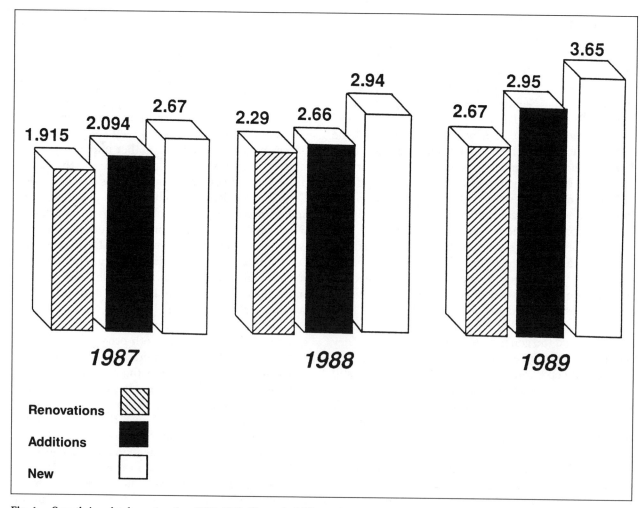

Fig. 1. Growth in school construction 1987–1989. Shown in billions of dollars.
Data from *American School and University* annual reports on educational construction, May 1988, 1989, 1990.

increase in school construction projects from 1987 through 1989.

The bibliographies and references in *Designing and Renovating School Library Media Centers* also reflect the scarcity of relevant titles on this topic, but give evidence of increasing interest in facilities planning.[6] Many architects and school administrators as well as school library media specialists are currently involved in facilities planning and construction programs, but have had little opportunity to focus systematically on a construction program for a school library media center. Winston Churchill observed that "we shape our buildings, thereafter they shape us."[7] Too often, poor planning and limited dialogue between the school and architectural teams leave educators with a facility that shapes the school library media program, rather than the reverse. This book is intended to assist the architectural team and the school planning team in the all-important dialogue necessary to provide school library media facilities that both "work" and make an architectural statement.

Summary of Contents

Chapter 1 gives an overview of the process, or framework, for facilities planning, from needs assessment through evaluation. A model for the development of an educational specifications document is presented in chapter 2. Chapter 3 is a description of the design process from the architect's perspective. Illustrative case studies of specific facilities can be found in chapters 4 and 5. Chapter 6 summarizes some of the human considerations and beneficial outcomes of good facilities planning. Appendixes supplement the case studies and offer additional helpful information.

Chapter 2 is the heart of the book. It presents a model for the educational specifications program statement. This document is the product of the school team's planning process; it provides the guide for the architectural team and becomes the springboard for dialogue between participants. Educational specifications have the major impact on the product of the architectural team's planning process—the physical structure that either impedes or facilitates delivery of a successful library media program. Educational specifications enable administrators and architectural firms to foresee program needs and to address appropriate questions to school library media specialists during the planning stages. The major objective is that resultant school library media facilities will have basic layouts that are timeless and that have inherent flexibility and the capacity to respond to future as well as present program needs.

References

1. Ralph E. Ellsworth and Hobart D. Wagener, *The School Library: Facilities for Independent Study in the Secondary School* (New York: Educational Facilities Laboratories, 1963). This report was edited by Ruth Weinstock, then a research associate at EFL.

2. Jane Anne Hannigan and Glenn E. Estes, *Media Center Facilities Design* (Chicago: American Library Association, 1978).

3. E. Blanche Woolls, "Facilities," in "Papers for the Treasure Mountain Research Retreat, Park City, Utah, October 17-18, 1989." Retreat ed. (Hi Willow Research and Publishing, 1989), 44-53; "Facilities," in *Information Power: Guidelines for School Library Media Programs*, prepared by the American Association of School Librarians and Association for Educational Communications and Technology (Chicago: American Library Association, 1988), 85-101. Two of the three selected readings (pp. 100+) were written in the mid-1970s.

4. For example, library restoration and renovation activities highlighted in "Inviting Places," *American Libraries* 21 (April 1990), were all public library projects.

5. Filomena Simora, ed., *The Bowker Annual of Library and Book Trade Information 1988.* 33d ed. (New York: R. R. Bowker, 1988), 365; Paul Abramson, "14th Annual Report on Educational Construction," *American School and University* 60 (May 1988): 16ff.

6. "Selected Readings" (pp. 000-000) and "Appendix G: State Publications on School Library Media Facilities" (pp. 000-000) contain a few titles from the eighties, most of recent vintage. For example, articles by a librarian, a library consultant, and an architect appeared in *School Library Journal* 36 (February 1990) as part of a feature highlighting the topic "A Blueprint for Effective Library Design."

7. Rhoda Tripp, ed., *International Thesaurus of Quotations* (New York: Crowell, 1970), 51.

ONE

The School Planning Team

The Planning Process

Planning for new or renovated school library media facilities should be a systematic process that begins with the informal recognition of needs and documentation of those needs through information gathering and formal assessment, followed by the development of an educational specifications document and a project proposal that is presented to the school board or other governing agency for approval. In the best of all possible worlds, this important initial work is the responsibility of a school planning team that consists of library media specialists, administrators, and other members of the school community.

When the project has been accepted, the school planning team finalizes the educational specifications document that will guide the design and construction program developed by the architectural team. Entry of the architect into the planning process depends on procedures for architect selection, the project timetable, and contractual guidelines created by the school district or other governing agency. Once hired, the architectural team uses the school team's educational specifications to develop graphic renderings of spaces and functions that gradually become more specific and detailed until a set of final construction drawings is completed.

These drawings will give contractors all the necessary data for the actual building work: creation of the shell (walls, floors, ceilings, windows, doors, etc.) and the internal systems (air, electrical, communications, etc.), as well as built-in furniture and special design features.

Inherent in the process is a continuing dialogue between the school planning team and the architectural team. Together they must review each stage of the project to be sure that expectations have been met and that work has been satisfactorily completed. They must also be able to communicate frequently to discuss unexpected problems and delays and any resulting changes or even to explore an exciting new design idea.

Selection of contractors is usually the result of a competitive bid process. Responsibility for monitoring work on the job site and for ensuring that building codes are being observed and that appropriate materials and methods are being used in accordance with contractual agreements and building plan specifications is the job of an appointed clerk of the works, or project manager, who is the school governing agency representative, and the architectural team. At the conclusion of construction, facilities must be inspected by both planning teams. The school team evaluates the completed

1

facility for its success in meeting educational expectations, while the architectural team evaluates on the basis of aesthetic, engineering, and construction standards.

The selection of new equipment, furniture, and shelving should be the school team's responsibility, in consultation with the architectural team. If the furniture and shelving are not part of the general contractor's construction contract, vendors and manufacturers are invited to bid for contracts to supply the desired items, which have been identified and described. The school planning team then analyzes the bids submitted and recommends contract awards.

Acceptance of the facility by the school team, the installation of furniture and shelving, the opening of the facility, and the subsequent evaluation of that facility complete the process and begin a new planning cycle.

Perhaps the most important step in the planning process is the initial identification of the key participants who will help shape the new facility's design and, ultimately, the program—the school planning team.

The Players

Whatever prompts identification of the need for new or renovated facilities, the planning process must involve those individuals who determine the school library media program—the library media staff, the district library media supervisor, the school's administration, the faculty, and student and community representatives. Together they must engage in the process from formal needs assessment through the construction documents and, ultimately, the completion of a facility integral to the school and its program. This planning team must be able to integrate its individual conceptions of a model school library media center with knowledge of the research, with experience and knowledge of the current program, and with recognition and understanding of emerging information resources and delivery systems. The planning team must also have a vision for the future and be able to anticipate such developments as changing emphases in collection balances between print and nonprint resources.

Perhaps one of the first assignments for the planning team would be to read selections from the futurists as well as from the literature describing "what is." In 1987, for example, Stewart Brand's *Media Lab* portrayed the future; today *Media Lab*

belongs to the literature of "what is."[1] Planning for facilities that anticipate change must take into consideration changes resulting from technology as well as changes in educational programming based on the needs of individuals who respond to the program, to expanding resources, and to the facility from intellectual, social, and psychological perspectives. Once the team has identified the basic assumptions that prompt a construction program and has established a future-oriented context for planning, the first phase of the planning process begins.

The First Play: Needs Assessment and Information Gathering

Needs assessment involves two processes: the gathering and synthesis of information to facilitate decision making, and the evaluation of programs and collections. The school planning team must become knowledgeable about a number of variables in order to adequately assess the needs of the educational program, of the students and teachers, and, therefore, of the library media component. If the project is to be replacement or renovation of an existing facility, then the team will evaluate the physical condition of that facility in terms of its ability to meet the current and future demands of collections and programs, as well as for the accommodation of newer information technologies.

There are a number of useful approaches to program evaluation and to collection analysis mentioned in the professional literature.[2] The team may wish to choose an instrument and modify it for the local setting, or even to create a new one. It is often useful to evaluate the existing facility and program by making a survey of users. Such a survey can also educate team members about current collections, services, and staffing patterns. If the project involves creating a new facility, the team may use a survey instrument to identify its own priorities for the new facility.

In either case the team must identify the educational goals and objectives to be achieved by the school library media program within the context of those established by the school and district. The team must examine current and projected demographics and identify curriculum trends and changes in teaching and learning styles as well as changes in accessing and using information. It must evaluate the existing or projected opening day collection and project changes in the balance between print and nonprint resources.

The group must be aware of the requirements, standards, and guidelines of the local school district or governing agency, the state department of education, the regional accrediting agency for schools, and such national professional organizations as the American Association of School Librarians (AASL) and the Association for Educational Communications and Technology (AECT).[3]

The needs assessment is the foundation for the school team's most important contribution to the planning process—the creation of a program statement, or educational specifications document, that projects the space requirements for the new or renovated facility in terms of educational goals and objectives and program needs and functions. This document will be the basis for the architectural design and construction phases of the project. With it the team may also submit a proposal that recommends a time frame of phases for funding, planning, and construction, and contains a rationale for the project that includes consideration of alternatives to new construction.

The Coach: The Library Consultant

The planning for the library media center should be coordinated by the school library media specialist with guidance from the district library media supervisor, who is often responsible for leadership in coordinating districtwide facilities planning. If the school's library media specialist has had little or no experience in construction programs and planning or if the district administrator recommends outside assistance, a school library media building consultant can be a cost-effective addition to the planning team. The consultant will have expertise in approaching a building program and will provide written comments as each phase evolves. This individual is supportive to the school library media specialist and/or district supervisor and helps facilitate the various phases of plan development. The consultant is involved in assessing the problem and will walk the planning team through gathering information and writing educational specifications.

The consultant may also review the documents and drawings for each phase with the school staff, assist in interpretation of the drawings, and suggest changes that reflect program and staff needs. The consultant assists in developing the furniture and shelving layout, bid specifications for furniture and shelving, the analysis of bid responses, and recommendations for awarding the bid. The consultant can provide further assistance in inspection of the facility, furniture, and shelving to identify problems in installation and in the quality of the workmanship. The contract with the consultant should delineate the services selected and the duration of the assistance.

The Game Plan: Educational Specifications

The information gathered in the needs assessment is now used to develop the program document, or educational specifications statement. This is a team effort under the leadership and editorship of the library media specialist, the district library media director, and the consultant. The educational specifications document describes the needs and the expectations of the school governing agency in clear language directed at lay people and architects, not in the language of the library profession. The audience for the document will be the school's administration and governing agency, facilities planning personnel, and, of course, the entire architectural team. Architects' knowledge of library media terminology is likely to be limited; clear, jargon-free language is imperative.

Architects often have difficulty understanding the variety of activities that occur simultaneously in the library media center facility. Audiovisual presentations, such as slide-tape or video programs developed for community groups or student orientations, can show the multiplicity of activities of a school library media center program. *The Information Power Video* produced by the Encyclopaedia Britannica (1988) is a good choice for this purpose. Visuals of features the team has identified as desirable are also helpful. Photos taken in other school library media centers and manufacturers' product descriptions also stimulate discussion. The use of such visuals is not to inhibit the architect's creativity but to provide a springboard for exploring possibilities.

The format of the program statement, or educational specifications document, will often be prescribed by the state's department of education. If there is to be construction or renovation of an entire building or portion of a building in addition to the library media center, the educational specifications for the library media center will be only one component of a larger document. The school's educational specifications document provides administrators, decision makers, and architects with the scope of the facility and the needs of each individual program and curricular area. The document also provides an understanding of the organizational and program structures.

The program statement should be sufficiently specific to provide design guidelines for the architectural firm, without becoming the design itself. The document should be descriptive, not prescriptive; the narrative should allow plenty of leeway for the creativity of the architect. For example, marketing is an important component of a successful library media program. Features that make the facility recognizable, invite entry, and generate interest, excitement, and participation are important considerations. The facility's design, which is the responsibility of the architectural firm, will help market the program within the school and the community. Therefore, the narrative should include a descriptive statement to remind the architect that such marketing is important and expected. The architect will answer with design features that call attention to the library media center, that set it apart, and that make it readily identifiable.

The educational specifications model presented in chapter 2 comprises eight sections. This sequence of topics imposes a process by which the planning team moves from broad to specific considerations as well as from textual to graphic and numeric representations of the desired facility. These eight sections may be grouped into two major functions: program description and special technical considerations.

Program Description

Sections I through VI discuss various aspects of the library media center program. Section I, organizational demographics, identifies the clientele served by the facility. Sections II and III describe the philosophy, or mission, of the program as well as goals and objectives. Section IV identifies educational, technological, and societal trends affecting both program and facility. Section V describes the variety of program activities that occur simultaneously in the library media center.

Section VI makes an important transition from narrative to graphic representations of program facilities, functions, and equipment. There is a brief description of the functions of the various physical spaces, which are then outlined in a facilities list. This is followed by a schematic rendering of these spaces in what is called a bubble diagram, adjacency diagram, or space chart.

The bubble diagram depicts the needed spaces and shows the special relationships and traffic flow of the various areas. Transferring conceptualization of the functions and the relationships of the spaces outlined in the facilities list to the bubble diagram assures that the team will have formulated its own understanding and philosophy of the functional relationships before any meeting with architects. Knowing what the program is and how it operates within the facility, then placing it in a diagram reduce the chance of confused signals both to administrative decision makers and to the architectural team. The bubble diagram will provide the architect with a visual understanding of the program's narrative description so critical for interpretation into a series of graphics that will document the entire construction program from the first schematic drawings through design development to the final construction drawings.

Special Considerations

Section VII contains a substantial number of specific technical recommendations and standards for various design components, including climate control, acoustical control, floor surfaces, walls, ceiling, lighting, windows, doors, water, communications, electrical control, safety, service drives and entrances, and built-in storage units.

Addressing special considerations as part of the program statement provides the architectural team with organizational and environmental requirements that may depart from the expected. These features make the difference between a functional library media center and one that creates problems for students, staff, collection development, and program implementation. It is appropriate to repeat statements in different areas of the document; members of the architectural team may miss some considerations if they turn only to the section that affects their own work. For example, electrical requirements may be described in a section on communications and then be repeated in other sections. Repetition reinforces the need for special considerations and assures that important design components get the appropriate attention.

Next Steps

Completion of the educational specifications statement is followed by school governing agency approval of the document and identification of funding sources. An architectural firm is then selected. School library media personnel usually are not involved in this process; architect selection will be a decision of the school governing agency or school administration.

An architectural firm's familiarity with design of school library media centers may have little influence on the selection process and a school planning team may find itself working with an inexperienced architect. The educational specifications for the library media center must, therefore, be definitive. It is critical that the program description provide a vignette of the entire library media program and various functions as well as activities of both students and staff. This description and additional visuals, as well as the section on special considerations, are key to the architectural firm's interpretation of the program into drawings that will produce a facility capable of meeting both present and future needs.

Models of educational specifications for a school library media program and facility can provide useful springboards for schools that anticipate new or renovated facilities. It is expected that the following model will be just that—a springboard. The school library media specialist who uses and adapts the model's format will find the interpretive comments helpful. The explanatory notes are separate from the model and are not part of the model itself. The model is not intended to be generic; there is no such panacea. Individual school or district specifications must reflect the needs of the unique school program, curriculum, community needs, geographic and climatic factors, and, most important, the personality of the educational community the school serves. In addition, there are often format requirements imposed by state agencies or district administration and facility departments. The educational specifications included here provide some direction to planners and the architectural team and furnish a basis for dialogue. Portions of the model may be adapted and expanded to meet the unique needs of individual schools and districts. Such adaptation should produce a program statement that meets the individual current and future needs of the school library media facility scheduled for construction or renovation.

References

1. Stewart Brand, *The Media Lab: Inventing the Future at MIT* (New York: Viking, 1987).

2. Shirley L. Aaron discusses approaches to program evaluation and summarizes the literature in "Measuring Services in *Information Power*," in *School Library Media Annual 1989, Vol. 7*, ed. Jane B. Smith (Englewood, Colo.: Libraries Unlimited, 1989), 3–20. James W. Liesener's *A Systematic Process for Planning Media Programs* (Chicago: American Library Association, 1976) is one of the early and most comprehensive approaches. See also AASL's *A Planning Guide for Information Power* (Chicago: American Library Association, 1988), and *Measures of Excellence for School Library Media Centers,* ed. David V. Loertscher (Englewood, Colo.: Libraries Unlimited, 1988) and pertinent sections in Loertscher's *Taxonomies of the School Library Media Program* (Englewood, Col.: Libraries Unlimited, 1988). Phyllis J. Van Orden summarizes the state of the art in "Evaluating the Collection," chap. 7 of her *Collection Program in Schools: Concepts, Practices, and Information Sources* (Englewood, Colo.: Libraries Unlimited, 1988), 253–271. See also *Collection Management for School Library Media Centers,* ed. Brenda H. White (New York: Haworth Press, 1986), and *Guide to the Evaluation of Library Collections,* ed. Barbara Lockett (Chicago: American Library Association, 1989).

3. AASL and AECT have cooperatively developed and published joint professional standards since 1969. The latest revision is *Information Power: Guidelines for School Library Media Programs* (Chicago: American Library Association, 1988).

Two

Educational Specifications
for the School Library
Media Center: A Model

I. Organizational Demographics

> This section provides the administrative decision makers and the architectural team with the numerical information needed for planning total square footage and budget allocations for the school library media center construction program.

Library media specialist–student ratio: _____
User capacity: _____
Total no. of library media specialists: _____
Total no. of support staff: _____
Grade levels or age levels for which program is intended: _____
Hours per day space will be used: _____
Off-calendar use of space: _____

II. Program Philosophy

> This section describes the program philosophy in general terms and sets the stage for the program perceptions that will inspire the decision makers and the architect.

The school library media center program and its environment are managed by the library media staff, skilled professionals who serve in different but often simultaneous roles as information specialists, teachers, and instructional consultants to provide an effective learning laboratory. Professional library media personnel encourage awareness of all the opportunities of the library media program. Instruction, guidance, assistance, and motivation are offered through resources and activities that promote lifelong learning. Locating, evaluating, and using information are taught as skills necessary to participate fully in a technological society. Through careful selection, planning, organization, and continuous reevaluation, library media specialists and support staff keep the collection and services of the library media center responsive to the long-range goals of the educational system as well as the immediate needs of the students and staff.

The library media center serves as the school's information center, providing resources and activities that enable students and staff to use ideas and information effectively as well as stimulate personal and intellectual growth. The library media center and its resources provide learning experiences, both active and passive, that will prepare students for success in an information age and ensure that students and staff are discriminating users of information and technology.

To meet the needs of its school, the library media program must provide appropriate resources and services. In addition to a variety of curriculum-oriented materials and equipment, there are many resources through which students may pursue personal and individual interests.

The school library media program must be flexible enough to accommodate groups of different sizes as well as individual instruction. Consistent with this commitment, students and staff must have the least restrictive access, both intellectually and physically, to library media materials and services.

III. Program Goals

This section turns the philosophy into program goals, establishes the classroom connection, and identifies the library media program with the teaching-learning process.

The library media program combines many resources, including people, services, materials, equipment, and facilities. Its major responsibility is to facilitate the teaching-learning process by providing access to resources and services to satisfy both the individual and instructional needs of students. The program creates an atmosphere that promotes inquiry, creativity, self-direction, communication of ideas, and the ability to use rational processes. The program provides an environment in which different learning styles can be accommodated and in which individuals and large and small groups can get information through a variety of media.

IV. Trends Affecting Facilities Design

This section focuses attention on how change affects facilities design. It provides the rationale for flexibility in design to ensure that the physical facility will meet the future program needs.

Changes in Information Technology

Rapid technological advances will continue to affect the procedures for locating information as well as those for circulation, inventory, and delivery of information. These advances will also affect the classroom connections to the media center. The rapidity with which technology is changing, especially the miniaturization of delivery systems, makes it difficult to predict what types of equipment and spatial accommodations will be needed in the future.

Automated systems accessed from individual workstations in the library media center, from stations in classrooms and teacher planning areas, and even from the homes of students and staff are now a reality. Information carriers—online public access catalogs, database workstations, instructional television, and so on—will either be centrally located in the library media center or accessed by telecommunications links from remote sites. Whatever the setup, learners will need the linking capacity the library media center facility provides with networks both inside and outside the building.

Facilities with built-in flexibility will allow the incorporation of new technology with minimum expense and disruption. Requirements to permit flexible use of a variety of audiovisual equipment, microcomputer equipment, and emerging technologies throughout the media center include adequate electrical outlets throughout the media center, not only on perimeter walls but throughout grids in the floor area or ceiling; conduit to carry telephone and television signals, or fiberoptics; and the ability to network stations served by common delivery systems. Flexibility requires a grid for distribution and networking of electronic equipment throughout the open floor space of the reading, listening, and viewing areas. Portable space dividers, freestanding shelving, and movable hanging-stack carrels are also essential elements of a flexible facilities plan.

Changes in Usage Patterns

Changing patterns of library media center use affect facilities planning. Day care, early childhood, and before- and after-school programs, and community use of facilities will require access to the library media center when school is not in session. Such off-calendar use of the facility and its resources affects the spatial relationship of the library media center to the entire school. The concept of year-round learning and the need to connect the school library media center to the community may require location of the center close to the perimeter of school and to access drives and parking areas. At the same time, the facility must remain central to classroom areas, encouraging interaction between the library media program and classroom learning activities.

Changes in Collection Size

Collection size and format adjust to the impact of the newer technologies, delivery systems, and changes in curriculum and instruction. The number and types of resources are responsive to changes in enrollment size. Curriculum changes that focus on student responsibility and independent learning alter the collection's format, scope, and size. A return to the inquiry approach to learning requires increases in collection size and scope. Emphasis on critical thinking requires a wider variety of materials and modes of delivery to meet individual learning styles and depth of inquiry. Cooperative learning activities create the need for more in-depth resources than did the cursory look at information resources of the back to basics movement.

Databases that traditionally occupied volumes in the area devoted to print materials alter collection size. Resources reside on laser discs 4½" in diameter and as thin as a file folder. Text that occupied bound volumes and rolls of microfilm is being transferred to laser disc formats to be read on computers at individual workstations. Replacement of text by computer simulations that enable faster comprehension of concepts precipitates reduction in collection size in some categories. In other categories, such as multicultural materials, the collection will increase. The ability to move and remove stacks and to replace traditional shelving with storage configurations yet unknown is critical to accommodate changing collection emphases and increasing demands for computer workstations. All this must be accomplished without altering library media space.

V. Program Activities

This section describes the different types of learning activities, both active and passive, that occur concurrently in the contemporary library media center. This concept is particularly difficult for architects to comprehend if they have had limited school library media experience.

The different program uses of the library media center's various areas can be observed in the activities that occur simultaneously:

- Individual students and teachers browse through computer databases
- Students study at carrels or work in small groups at tables
- Teachers and library media specialists instruct large and small groups of students in the use of library media resources and their accompanying technologies
- Students view and listen to live dramatic presentations, such as puppet shows, role playing, and storytelling
- Students use computers to access information services beyond their own school library media center
- Teachers consult with the library media staff to select appropriate materials for teaching curriculum units
- Students work with teachers and library media staff on television productions to be distributed throughout the school
- Students and teachers create visuals in the production area
- Groups of students engage in search activities
- Community volunteers listen to students read aloud
- Staff participate in professional growth activities and learn the use of new technologies
- Adult volunteers serve as mentors assisting students in research
- Library media center staff create displays and exhibits that market the center's program and resources
- Students participate in teleconferences or communicate with authors or other famous personalities through computers
- Students listen to or view audiovisual programs in small groups
- Library media staff circulate, retrieve, and store the audiovisual and communications equipment
- Library media staff make minor repairs and maintain equipment
- Library media staff ship and receive materials and equipment.

Both planned and spontaneous interaction in the library media center can occur concurrently. The library media center program is action-centered: It facilitates attainment of knowledge by both individuals and groups using different learning modes and different technologies for transmitting information. As a learning laboratory, the library media center must provide flexibility to permit participation in both active and quiet ways.

VI. Program Facilities, Functions, and Equipment

This section concludes the general narrative statements and precedes the specifics required for space allocation, types of facilities, and special conditions within the school library media center.

A contemporary library media center provides the space and resources for a variety of dissimilar activities to occur simultaneously. The center should include features that will market both the program and the facility to the school and to the community. The library media center should be recognizable and invite entry. It should have features that will generate interest and stimulate students and teachers to participate in the activities it offers.

Location

The library media facility should be centrally located with easy access from all instructional areas of the school as well as from exterior areas, access drives, and parking. In multiple-story structures, the center should be located near an elevator to accommodate the physically handicapped and to facilitate transport of heavy audiovisual equipment and delivery of shipments. The provision of rest rooms for staff and patrons is important, particularly if the library media center is used during off-calendar hours when school is not in regular session. The key to good design is the inherent flexibility that allows a multiplicity of activities, accommodates changes and new emphases in curriculum, provides for changing technology, and permits a traffic flow that minimizes interruptions and distractions.

Space Allocation

The assignment of physical space to program functions is critical to effective use of the library media center by students and teachers and to effective delivery of program by the library media center staff. Strategic location of program functions within the total allocated square footage will market the program and facilitate the effective use of staff time. The spatial relationships within the center provide for efficient flow of traffic; the inherent flexibility in the center allows for change and easy adaptation of spaces; and the center's aesthetics stimulate a positive response to the work environment. All respond to the school's total program and will serve to market the library media program to both the school and external communities.

Planning for the library media center's physical space allocations must be conjunctive to the total school program. It must reflect the regional accreditation and state standards for square footage, seating, and program functions and should also reflect the current national guidelines presented in *Information Power.*[1]

The Space Chart

Differences in school programs, levels, and specific communities served will affect the spatial relationships and allocations in the design of any library media facility. These relationships are depicted on a space chart, or "bubble diagram" (see fig. 2). Spatial relationships and the amount of square footage allocated will also reflect criteria in state planning guidelines and the program philosophy of individual districts and schools. For example, elementary school diagrams may include a story/presentation area. Secondary school space charts may show carrel areas or computer workstations in carrel-like configurations within the large open area. Special education centers may have sections of wall space for sensory activities and manipulatives. Some space charts may include computer-assisted instruction laboratories. Others will eliminate production facilities and place these facilities in a district center. The space chart will depict those areas selected for inclusion in the school library media center by the school planning team.

The diagram will show spatial relationships and proportionate sizes of individual areas to the whole. Whether ovals, circles, or some other geometric forms are used, the message relayed by the bubble diagram will be understood by the architectural team. See Appendix A for an explanation of the construction of a bubble diagram.

The Facilities List

The facilities list will reflect the nomenclature assigned the different library media center spaces by the state department of education or governing body. Department of education guidelines usually define space terminology and present a range of square footage allocations for these spaces. It is from these that administrators and school board or governing agencies select the spaces and allocations to meet the individual school or district's program requirements. Private and independent schools have greater latitude in such choices as they do not have to meet the requirements imposed on publicly supported institutions. A list of state documents that, as of 1989, contain such guidelines is included in Appendix G.

Part of the initial planning process requires the school planning team to investigate state requirements and nomenclature. The model's facilities list reflects the spaces depicted in *Information Power*'s schematic representation of spaces as found in figure 2. Educational specifications developed for the individual school construction project should include the facilities list at this point (see table 1). The list should include four parts: (1) the spaces according to the nomenclature assigned; (2) the functions, activities, and special considerations; (3) the special furniture and equipment; and (4) the square footage allocated the area according to the parameters established by the governing agency. The fourth part, a column that presents the square footage allocation, has been omitted from the model because individual square footage assignments will vary. See Appendix C for a suggested basic equipment checklist that can be used to identify equipment for the facilities list.

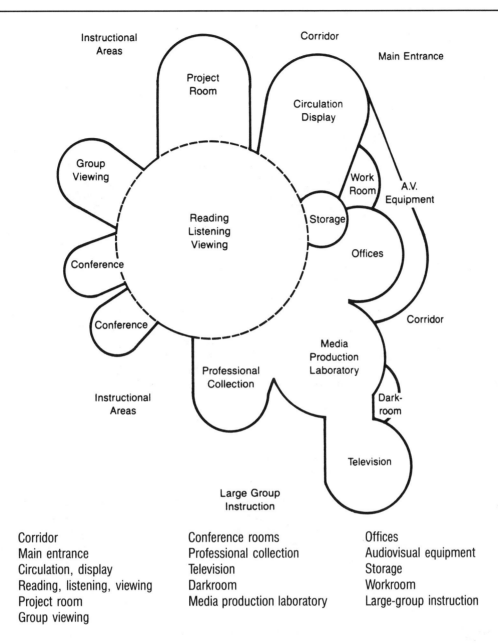

Corridor
Main entrance
Circulation, display
Reading, listening, viewing
Project room
Group viewing

Conference rooms
Professional collection
Television
Darkroom
Media production laboratory

Offices
Audiovisual equipment
Storage
Workroom
Large-group instruction

Fig. 2. Schematic representation of spaces by location.
Reprinted by permission of the American Association of School Librarians and Association for Educational Communications and Technology, from *Information Power: Guidelines for School Library Media Program* (Chicago: American Library Association, 1988), 90.

Table 1. Facilities List

Library Media Center Spaces	Functions/Actitivies/ Special Considerations	Special Furnishings/ Equipment
Main entrance, circulation, display	Provides space for traffic control, opportunity to market the school library media program to the school and community. Provides physical access to library media center. Will provide adequate space for checking materials in and out. Should provide access for handicapped.	Circulation desk Computer workstation and printer Copy machine Display cases Electronic security gates
Reading, listening, viewing	Provides shelving to house collection of print and nonprint materials. Shelving may define areas to accommodate different sized groups and functions. Seating for individuals and for groups of different sizes should be available in areas defined by shelving. Visible control by library media center personnel is consideration.	Carrels (freestanding and hanging-stack) CD-ROM terminals and printers OPAC workstations and printers Microform reader/printers Microform cabinets Atlas stand Dictionary stand Tables Chairs Lounge furniture Shelving
Project room	Provides area for production of visuals, models, sound recordings. Should be accessible by large groups without disrupting activities in reading/browsing/listening area, and visible from areas staffed by library media center personnel.	Built-in cabinets with locks Island counter with built-in light tables Cabinets and drawers of varying sizes beneath Work surface counters with recessed and dropped areas to accommodate computers and typewriters Refrigerator Sinks
Group viewing	Provides classroom-size area for different types of presentations and instruction. Should accommodate the use of all types of media and accommodate teleconferences. Visual control by library media center personnel.	Lecture tables Chairs Podium Screen (wall or rear view) Televisions
Conference areas	Multipurpose areas under supervision of library media personnel. Acoustics provide for use of audio-visual equipment; portable typewriter/computer table. Movable walls provide for flexible use by different sized groups.	Chairs Conference tables Counter with built-in cabinets and locks Television

Library Media Center Spaces	Functions/Actitivies/ Special Considerations	Special Furnishings/ Equipment
Professional collection	Provides storage area for professional books and periodicals. Conference and planning area used by small groups or individual teachers. Area for previewing, selecting, evaluating print and nonprint materials and equipment.	Carrels (wet) Shelving Chairs Tables Computers Telephone modem
Television	Provides space for students and teachers engaged in production and distribution of programs to classrooms, auditorium, cafeteria, library media center carrels, and conference areas. Convenient access to media production laboratory, equipment storage, and reading/listening/viewing areas. Should be accessible by groups without disrupting activities in reading/browsing/listening area. Includes area for production of sound recordings. Must be soundproof and provide area for editing and distribution of audio and video programs. Should be secure.	Built-in cabinets with locks Television cameras Tripods, dollies Video decks Mixers Microphones Track lighting Audio recording equipment Editing equipment Head end equipment Amplifiers Table Chairs Counter work surfaces
Darkroom	Provides production work surface and storage facilities for individual students and small group use. Adjacent to media production laboratory.	Enlarger Photo processing sink Drying rack Counter with built-in cabinets for storage
Media production laboratory	Provides area for production of visuals, models, sound recordings. Locate adjacent to equipment storage area. Should be accessible by groups without disrupting activities in reading/browsing/listening area, and visible from areas staffed by library media center personnel.	Built-in cabinets with locks Island counter with built-in light tables Cabinets and drawers of varying sizes beneath Work surface counters with recessed and dropped areas to accommodate computers and typewriters Refrigerator Sinks
Offices	Provide areas for quiet work by professional staff. Will accommodate interviews and planning with teachers.	Desk Chairs Cabinets Shelving

Continued

Table 1 *continued*

Library Media Center Spaces	Functions/Actitivies/ Special Considerations	Special Furnishings/ Equipment
Audiovisual equipment	Provides storage for small and large equipment on shelves or rolling projection carts, parts for repairs, consumable supplies, lamps; counter height cabinetry and work surfaces to facilitate routine maintenance and minor repair of equipment. Location should be near corridors, loading docks, elevator. Area should be secure.	Built-in cabinets with locks Shelving Stools Tables Test equipment
Workroom	Area for technical processing and repair of materials, used by staff. Adjacent to entrance, circulation, display, media production laboratory. Includes periodical storage shelving. Physical and visual access to other support and production areas of library media center. Provides storage area for back issues of magazines. Located near areas staffed by library media center personnel.	Built-in cabinets, drawers, desk, storage areas Shelving Desks for library media center personnel Computers Fax equipment Copy equipment Sinks Carrels (wet) Chairs Tables
Large-group instruction	Provides large area for different types of presentations and instruction for groups larger than a class. Should accommodate the use of all types of media and accommodate teleconferences. Visual control by library media personnel.	Lecture tables Chairs Podium Screen (wall or rear view) Televisions

VII. Special Considerations

Special considerations address the organizational and environmental requirements that depart from the norm but are critical to the successful operation of library media programs. Special considerations will reflect the specific needs generated by local geographic and climatic conditions.

Climate Control

While climate control can be accomplished in a variety of ways, from cross ventilation to entire energy management systems, maintenance of the humidity at 60% is essential to the preservation of materials and equipment in all climates. This level of moisture prevents drying out of materials in heated facilities and the growth of molds and mildew in more humid areas.

The entire library media center should have a climate control system for air and heat. It is important that the library media center have a separate, independent heating/cooling system that can be regulated to control the temperature and humidity so critical to the handling, storage, and preservation of materials and equipment. An independent climate control system permits use of the library media center for off-calendar events, such as summer reading programs. Windows should enable exchange of fresh air and provide ventilation when the climate control system is not in use.

Humidity must be maintained at a maximum of 60% at all times by means of the following systems:

a. The normal heating/air conditioning system for this area is to maintain temperature and humidity during periods when the area is occupied and is to be controlled by the building energy management system.

b. Separate humidifying/dehumidifying equipment is to maintain a maximum of 60% relative humidity when the area is unoccupied and the normal air conditioning is off. This is to be controlled by the energy management system.

c. Air conditioning units should have electrostatic filters.

The temperature must be maintained at a maximum level of 70°–77° F. with humidity at 60% in the library media center.

In areas used for equipment storage and maintenance, television and audio studios, and in the telecommunications distribution area, the temperature is to be maintained at a set point of 76° F., +/− 1° F. when the areas are in use. This is accomplished by the building air conditioning/heating and ventilation system. A control to limit temperature at 76° F. as an absolute is necessary. This temperature control is also required in the television studio when there is use of high wattage studio lighting.

Supply and return air vents should be located high on the walls or in the ceiling with air velocities low enough to prevent problems created by moving papers, hair, or clothing. Supply and return air vents should not create noise in production areas. Sound from any subsystem of the overall air conditioning system should not be picked up on the audio during productions.

The darkrooms should be separately vented. Exhaust fans with light-tight louvers must be vented directly to the exterior of the building.

Rest rooms should have forced ventilation to the outside and have a control and light switch. Lights should start instantly.

Since wall space for shelving is a primary concern, return air vents should be positioned high on walls (at least 86″ from floor) or installed in the ceiling.

Acoustical Control

Attention should be given to the acoustics in all areas. Acoustical drop ceilings in all areas are generally preferred.

The conference rooms should be provided with sufficient acoustical treatment to prevent external noise sources from interfering with recordings. Walls in both the television studio area and conference rooms should have special acoustical treatment to facilitate recording. Mechanical equipment rooms and air handling equipment should be accessed from the exterior of the library media center and have sound barriers to isolate noise and vibrations. Air handling units should be removed from reading/listening/viewing areas and from entrance/circulation areas and should have provision for reduction of vibration when in operation. Air conditioning vents should be low velocity to minimize ambient noise.

Floor Surfaces

Carpeting should be continuous where equipment is moved on rolling carts, and is required in the following areas:

- Circulation, display area
- Reading, listening, viewing
- Group viewing
- Conference rooms
- Professional collection
- Offices
- Workroom area
- Large-group instruction area

Carpeting in the area of the circulation desk should have extra padding.

Vinyl or tile flooring is recommended for all other areas and in areas where running water is used:

- Main entrance
- Project room
- Television studio area
- Telecommunications distribution areas
- Darkroom
- Media production laboratory
- Audiovisual equipment storage, distribution, and maintenance areas

The main entrance to the library media center, a high traffic area, may be of durable material, such as quarry tile or nonskid ceramic tile.

Walls

All walls should be finished with a tackable surface and provide ample area for display of student projects and artwork. Neutral colors on the wall surfaces will allow the many colors of the student projects and the library materials to brighten the rooms.

Signage and limited graphics to highlight areas can be part of the overall design.

If the facility's elevation is one story and adjacent to classroom areas, the walls surrounding the media center and the area for equipment storage, distribution, and maintenance should be designed to extend above the drop ceiling to the roof to prevent unauthorized entry into these areas through the ceiling crawl space.

One wall of the television studio is to be painted light blue to provide the television production backdrop.

Walls in the television studio and conference rooms should have special acoustical treatment to facilitate recording.

The audiovisual storage room will include 20 square feet of pegboard with fasteners mounted to the wall.

Walls between conference rooms should include folding or movable walls to facilitate change in size of conference facilities.

Walls between the largest patron area and support areas shall include observation windows beginning at least 45" from floor, leaving space for shelving and carpeting beneath. Observation windows should be in appropriate areas to provide visual control by staff from circulation and support areas. All windows must be placed to accommodate wall-mounted shelving running in 3' increments.

Ceiling

Standard acoustical tile should be used in all areas.

Lighting

Light control blinds are required for observation windows and those architectural features that provide natural light or those designed to aesthetically enhance the library media center.

Separate light controls should be provided for each room or area in the library media center and should be located at each door or entrance inside the room or area. A keyed master switch controlling light for the entire media center should be located near the staff exit to enable all areas to be darkened simultaneously.

Lighting fixtures should be located for uniform illumination.

Security lights, which operate when regular lights are turned off or during power outages, should be strategically placed to light a clear path from all support areas, but they must be placed in areas that are removed from projection screens. Lighted exit signs for emergency evacuation and exit should be placed for maximum visibility.

Red "In-Use" lights should be located outside entrance doors to darkrooms and television studios.

Special lens systems should shield light fixtures in areas housing computers. Fixtures can be shielded by such systems as paracube or parabolic lenses. Lighting is to be zoned to permit banks to be switched off in separate areas of large, open spaces.

Adjustable track lighting (two 16' tracks) is to be installed in the closed-circuit television production area.

Where ambient light will affect the use of front projection audiovisual equipment, a rearview screen will be necessary.

Windows

Exterior Windows. Provision must be made for fresh air exchange, and windows that open should be included where possible. Since wall-mounted shelving is of primary importance, the majority of the exterior windows should begin at least 86" from the floor and take a minimum of wall space. Consideration should be given to alternative methods of providing natural light through the use of such architectural features as glass brick or skylights. Limited decorative windows can be placed near entrances and can provide visual access to scenic exterior areas. Decorative windows may also be located throughout the facility if placed to accommodate standard 3' lengths of shelving and a sufficient number of linear feet of shelving to accommodate the collection. Light-control blinds must be provided in all areas of the library media center where natural light enters in order to facilitate projection by audiovisual equipment.

There should be no windows of any kind in the television studio and telecommunications areas.

Observation Windows. With the exception of the audiovisual equipment storage, distribution, and maintenance room, all other areas should be observable from both the center of the facility and the circulation area. Observation windows should be in all commonly shared walls. Observation windows must begin at least 45" from the floor to permit the installation of shelving beneath, and must not interrupt the 3' increments required for continuous linear footage of shelving. The minimum window width should be 72". Maximum window size is determined by the final library media center design and required built-ins. Only clear, tempered, or reinforced glass or plexiglass is acceptable.

Doors

Doors should have quiet operating mechanisms and should be light enough in weight and design to be opened easily by students. To assure safe transport of heavy audiovisual equipment on carts, all doors should be installed without thresholds.

The work area and media production laboratory should have one door to a service corridor for deliveries.

Special attention should be given to hardware and security considerations. The service corridor should open to the exterior of the library media center. Screens for the book electronic security system will be located at the main entrance/exit doors.

Water

No water fountains should be located in main reading, listening, viewing, or stack areas.

The workroom should be equipped with a sink having a raised gooseneck faucet, providing hot and cold water.

The media production laboratory area and project room should have a double sized sink without a divider. The sink should be equipped with a raised gooseneck faucet, providing hot and cold water.

Sinks shall be at one end of built-in counters.

All sinks should be equipped with liquid soap and paper towel dispensers.

Communications Networks

This section addresses communications networks, such as closed-circuit television systems, that are internal to the building. Although these systems may link with district systems or communitywide systems, such as cable television, the model addresses only the internal communications network of the school.

Television System. The television distribution system originates in the distribution area of the library media center and extends to all classrooms and instructional areas. It is a multichannel system capable of local origination or playback of programming on videotape decks and/or redistribution of special programs from the television antenna serving the building.

All "head-end" equipment is mounted in a television equipment rack in the telecommunications distribution area. Included in the head-end equipment will be a downconverter power supply, a VHF/UHF channel converter, individual channel amplifiers, television modulators, and all necessary splitters, mixers, and filters to complete the distribution system.

The cable distribution system is to be installed with connecting outlets throughout the library media center and in all classrooms, administrative areas, the auditorium, and the cafeteria.

All television cable outlets must be installed no more than 6" from 110-volt electrical service outlet boxes and should be no more than 5' from the floor. Closed-circuit television cable and 110-volt supply must be in separate boxes. Location of these boxes should be clear of traffic patterns.

Television signals broadcast from the district instructional television center will be received at the antenna tower serving the building. To minimize signal loss through long antenna lead-in cables, the tower should be located close to the library media center. It must be designed and positioned to permit easy maintenance. Coaxial cables connect the antenna to the power supplies and amplifying equipment in the telecommunications distribution area. Conduits sufficient to handle half-inch coaxial cables should be provided between the tower location and the distribution center. Antennae and/or cable for receiving local television channels shall be included.

Projection Screens. One 60" × 60" ceiling-mounted electric projection screen with modular motor, low-voltage multiple switching, matte finish, and keystone elimination capacity is to be installed in areas designated for large-group instruction and group viewing.

If ambient light inhibits the use of front projection equipment, a plexiglass rearview screen with protective coating should be installed.

Intercom System. As part of the school's communication system, two-way communication from each classroom and instructional area of the school to the library media center is required for better use of the instructional television and library media center resources. The system must include a call-in box in each classroom and a response unit in the library media support area closest to the circulation desk.

Clocks. There should be a clock in each room of the library media center.

Telephone System. Modular telephone outlets, compatible with the school system's telephone equipment, should be provided in the circulation area, the offices, workroom, media production laboratory, and storage areas.

A dedicated telephone line is required in areas closest to the circulation desk to facilitate use of a telephone modem and computers. This line will also serve the catalog area and carrels housing microcomputers. Provisions should be made in the grid system to link telephone lines throughout the library media center. Location must be per working drawings that locate carrels, computer stations, circulation desk, and furniture installations requiring networking.

Computers. The computerized library circulation, inventory, and public access catalog system uses computers located in the support areas, at the circulation desk, and in workstations used by students and teachers. There should be provision for a printer to serve each workstation.

Grid System and Outlets. A grid system designed on a 10-foot-square grid will be in the floor to accommodate electrical service, television, and communications distribution throughout area.

The grid system should provide for linkage among the support areas, the circulation area, and workstations. The grid system should be large enough to carry electric power, computer networking cables, and telephone lines and provide for elimination of interference or "cross-talk." Access panels for installation of outlets will be on 10-foot centers at minimum. Location and number of floor outlets will be according to the working drawings that locate carrels, computer stations, circulation desk, and other furniture installations requiring electrical service and networking.

Floor outlets should be of brass construction, flush to the floor, with hinged covers opened with a single key. Electric outlets along walls should be located at 10-foot intervals. Electric outlets should be in all support columns. Electric outlets should be located at a minimum of 5-foot intervals along all work counters.

Double duplex electrical outlets, each with dedicated circuits, should be installed at each of the proposed computer workstations in the library media center, per working drawings.

Double duplex electrical outlets, each on dedicated circuits, and a telephone jack should be installed at the circulation desk area.

Dedicated circuits should be labeled, for example, "computer outlet."

Electrical Control

Electrical considerations addressed in the preceding section, "Communications Networks," are repeated in this section devoted entirely to the topic of electrical requirements. The inclusion under "Communications Networks" is necessary because of the interrelationships of those major considerations and the possibility that members of large architectural firms may study only those areas of the educational specifications that relate to their own work assignments.

Since wall space for shelving is of primary concern, all electrical switches, fire alarm controls, intercom switches, thermostats, and other electrical controls should be concentrated vertically to use as little wall space as possible. No control should be located behind shelving-unit upright supports.

In all areas, 110-volt duplex wall outlets are to be installed every 10 feet on available wall space.

In addition to wall outlets, 110-volt duplex floor outlets are to be installed throughout the reading, browsing, listening, viewing, and stack areas in a grid system designed on a 10-foot-square grid. The system provides for the installation of 110-volt electrical service, television, and communication cables. Access panels for installation of outlets are to be on 10-foot centers. Duplex floor outlets are to be located to accommodate furniture placement shown on working drawings. Floor outlets should be of brass construction, flush to the floor, with hinged covers accessed by a single key.

The computerized library circulation, inventory, and catalog system uses computers located in the support areas, at the circulation desk, and at workstations in the reading, listening, and viewing area. There should be provision for printers to serve these workstations.

Dedicated 110-volt surge-suppressed circuit isolation transformer/voltage regulators are to be located at the circulation desk and catalog areas for the computers. Dedicated outlets should be labeled, for example, "computer outlet."

Double duplex electrical outlets, each with a dedicated circuit, should be installed at each computer workstation in the library media center as per working drawings. Double duplex electrical outlets, each on dedicated circuits, and a telephone jack should be installed at the circulation desk area.

Closed-circuit television antenna outlets (six inches from 110-volt electrical service) should be located throughout the reading, listening, viewing, and stack areas to accommodate furniture placement on the working drawings.

Areas with built-in counters should have 110-volt strip outlets at 5-foot intervals: media production laboratory, workroom, periodical storage, professional collection (teacher/professional area), television and audio studios, telecommunications distribution, and so on. Outlets should be installed the full length of the counters, with no outlets placed within 1 foot of either side of the sinks.

The cable distribution system is to be installed with connecting outlets throughout the library media center, and in all classrooms, administrative areas, the auditorium, and the cafeteria.

All television cable outlets must be installed no more than 6″ from 110-volt electrical service outlet boxes and should be no more than 5′ from the floor. Closed-circuit television cable and 110-volt supply must be in separate boxes. The location of these boxes should be clear of traffic patterns.

One 60″ × 60″ ceiling-mounted electric projection screen with modular motor, low-voltage multiple switching, matte finish, and keystone elimination capacity is to be installed in the large-group instruction area.

Safety

Local codes will determine the types of safety issues that should be addressed here. The type of building materials, the location of exits, and whether turnstiles can be installed are the architectural firm's responsibility to determine. Plans are to be drawn in compliance with local codes.

Some safety issues are covered elsewhere in the educational specifications. For example, when power failures occur and climate control systems shut down, it is important to have access to change of air and good ventilation. Other safety issues may be dealt with at another stage in the design process. For example, parents of handicapped students frequently oppose the placement of library media centers above the first floor. Elevators stop functioning in an emergency, leaving handicapped students with mobility problems unable to evacuate rapidly.

Adequate aisle space between stacks and freestanding furniture is necessary to ease the movement of handicapped individuals and the movement of loaded book trucks and audiovisual carts. A minimum of 3′ of space should be allowed between stacks. A minimum of 4′ should be left between tables in nontraffic areas, and 6′ between tables in traffic areas. Leg room should be positioned away from aisle areas.

When fire extinguishers are being installed, consideration for the conservation of wall space and the 3-foot increments for shelving is important. Extinguishers should be placed at the ends of ranges of wall-mounted shelving for quick visual location and to prevent breaks in the ranges.

The television antenna tower must be designed and located to provide proper and safe access for maintenance personnel and, at the same time, prevent climbing by students and other unauthorized personnel.

Service Drives and Entrances

Whenever possible, service drives should supply the core area of the library media center and facilitate delivery of materials and equipment.

If a self-supporting, freestanding, ground-mounted concrete pole is used to support the television antennae, the service drives must provide accommodation for a large bucket truck to access the area.

Built-in Storage Units

Built-in storage units are defined as millwork or cabinetwork and are usually custom designed to fit the individual configuration of the library media center. These items are included in the general contractor's construction contract, as opposed to freestanding equipment and furniture that is bid and purchased by the school organization.

Finish on all built-in units should be high-pressure laminate (.050 with .050 backing, simultaneously applied) with a minimum of ¾" thickness.

Storage Cabinets

Built-in cabinets will consist of several basic types that will vary in combination according to the linear feet of an available wall space:

Type A: Drawer storage unit (fig. 3). Forty-inch unit is to consist of two vertical rows of drawers with varying depths, the bottom drawer being the

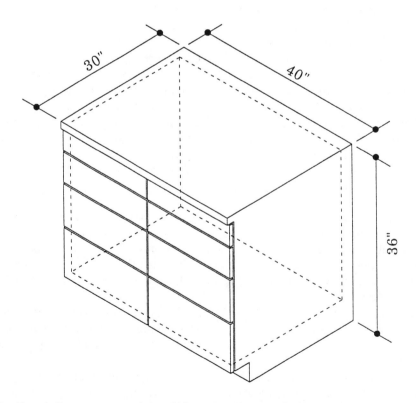

Fig. 3. Type A: Drawer storage unit (36" high × 40" wide × 30" deep)

deepest (10-inch vertical depth) and the top drawer the shallowest (4½-inch vertical depth). All drawers are to be mounted on metal roller guides. Minimum drawer width is to be 16". Drawers should have interior adjustable dividers. Counter depth is to be 30".

Type B: Drawer/closed shelving unit. Forty-inch unit consists of a closed-door cabinet with one interior, adjustable shelf (see fig. 4). Vertical adjustment of the shelf is to be in 1-inch increments. Immediately below the counter top and above the closed cabinet area are two 4½-inch vertical-depth drawers the width of each cabinet door. Drawers are to be mounted on metal roller guides. Counter depth is to be 30".

Type C: Wide drawer unit. Forty-inch unit is to consist of a vertical arrangement of wide, shallow drawers for the storage of flat pictures, charts, and other visuals (see fig. 5). The minimum width of drawers is to be 40". The maximum vertical depth of all drawers is to be 3". Drawers are to be mounted on metal roller guides. Counter depth is to be 30".

Type D: Computer desk unit. Forty-eight-inch unit must include a 26-inch-high work surface, minimum of 22"d × 23"w (see fig. 6). Kneehole width is to be a minimum of 24". One vertical row of drawers is to be below the work surface. Drawers are to be of varying vertical depth (10-inch maximum) and mounted on metal roller guides. Counter depth is to be 30".

Type E: Desk unit. Forty-eight-inch unit is to consist of a desk height (30") work surface and two adjacent, shallow drawers below the work surface

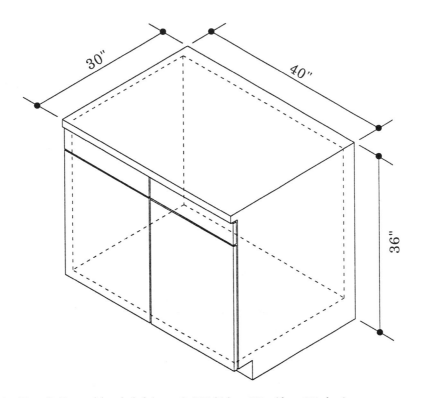

Fig. 4. Type B: Drawer/closed shelving unit (36" high × 40" wide × 30" deep)

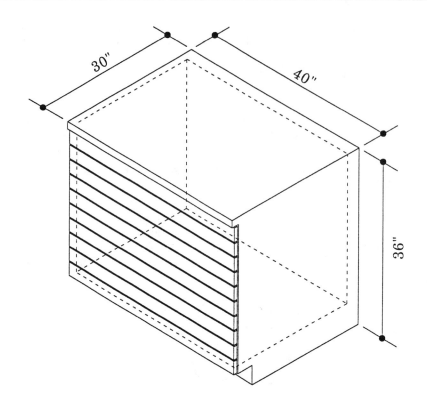

Fig. 5.   Type C: Wide drawer unit (36″ high × 40″ wide × 30″ deep)

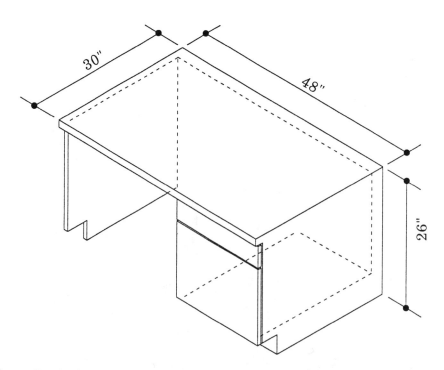

Fig. 6.   Type D: Computer desk unit (26″ high × 48″ wide × 30″ deep)

(see fig. 7). Maximum drawer width is to be 20". Vertical drawer depth is to be a maximum of 4½". Kneehole width is to be a minimum of 24". Counter depth is to be 30".

Type F: Island counter.   This unit is to be accessible for work from all sides (see fig. 8). Approximate overall dimensions are 12' long × 6' wide × 3' high. Counter will have raised area above center for double duplex outlets on each side. Each end of the unit is to have one vertical row of wide drawers for the storage of poster board and other graphic art supplies. Maximum vertical depth of all drawers is to be 3". Minimum width of drawers is to be 44". Minimum horizontal depth of drawers is to be 44". All drawers are to be installed with metal roller guides. Cabinet with one adjustable shelf will supply each side of center.

Type G: Vertical map cabinet.   The cabinet should be designed to hold 30 maps in the vertical position (see fig. 9). Cabinet must provide enough space to accommodate rolled maps from 4" to 7" in diameter and 68" high. Storage unit should provide visual and physical accessibility to maps at rear.

Work Counter
The workroom area (with the exception of space required for the library shelving units, a 4-foot open space for the catalog, and space for file cabinets) should have a work counter with a combination of closed cabinets and drawer storage units beneath (types A and B), and closed cabinets with one adjustable shelf above. This cabinetry should be placed along all available wall space. A sink should be installed at one end of the counter. Two desk units (one each of types D and E) should be located beneath the observation window.

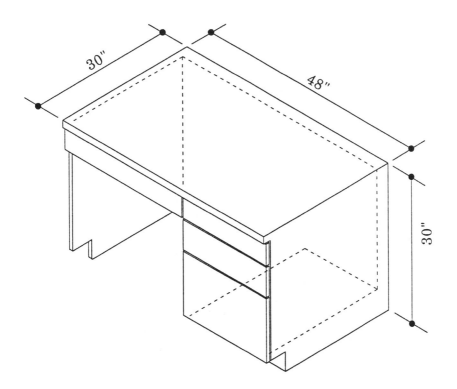

Fig. 7.   Type E: Desk unit (30" high × 48" wide × 30" deep)

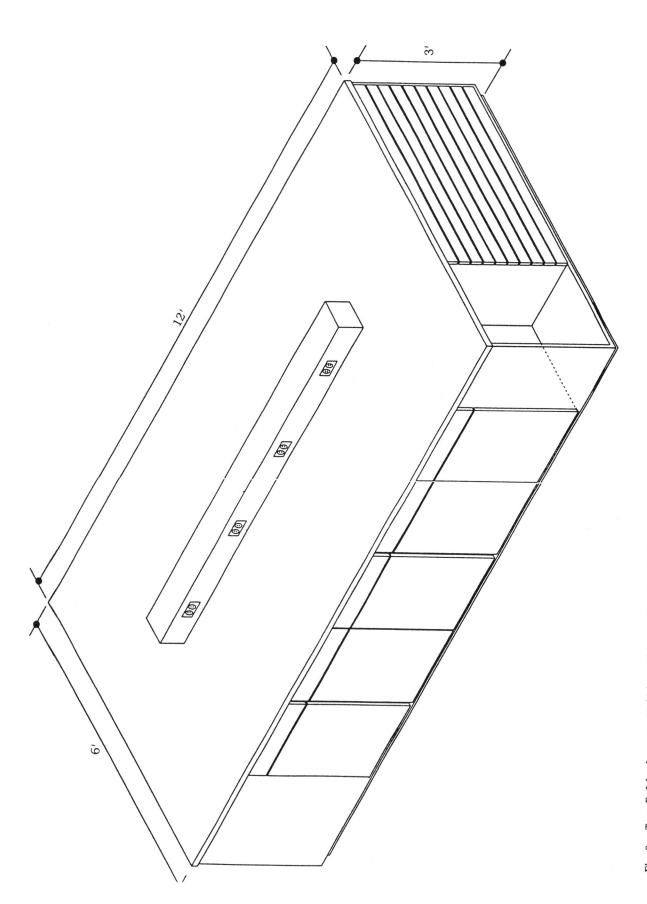

Fig. 8. Type F: Island counter (3' high × 12' long × 6' wide; 44-inch-deep, back to-back counters with 4-inch raised center section for electrical outlets)

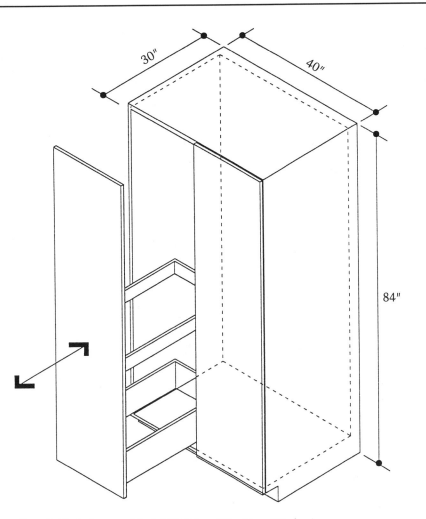

Fig. 9. Type G: Vertical map cabinet (84″ high × 40″ wide × 30″ deep)

The media production laboratory should have a work counter approximately 17′ in length installed along one wall. (Counter is to consist of alternating type A, B, C, and E units.) A second counter, approximately 12′ with type B cabinets below, will include a sink to be installed at one end of the counter. Closed cabinets with adjustable shelves are to be located 24″ above all counter tops. An island counter (type F) is to be accessible for work from all sides and is positioned in the center of the media production laboratory and the project room. A vertical map cabinet (type G) for storage of rolled wall maps should be near work counters along wall. All cabinets and drawers in the 17-foot counter are to have locks controlled by one master key.

Cabinets

The periodical storage area shall include one work counter (minimum 12′) with a combination of closed cabinets and drawer storage units (one type A and three type B). Closed cabinets with one adjustable shelf 18″ deep should be placed above the counter. This configuration should be close to the entrance and within reasonable distance of the circulation desk area to facilitate retrieval of periodicals. Periodicals will be stored on wall-mounted or freestanding shelving as described in the following section, "Library Shelving."

The telecommunications distribution area will include a 6-foot work counter (minimum) with a combination of closed cabinets and drawer storage units (types A and B). This unit should be located next to the closed-circuit television distribution unit. Lockable cabinets (3 linear feet long and 84" high) with 12-inch wide adjustable shelving and accessible with one master key will be placed along the wall and next to the work counter.

The vertical map cabinet should be designed to hold 30 maps in the vertical position. Compartments must be wide enough to accommodate rolled maps from 4" to 7" in diameter and 68" high. The storage unit should provide visual and physical accessibility to maps at rear. This cabinet is to be installed in the media production laboratory.

Library Shelving

If the collection integrates print and nonprint in the stack area, shelving shall be 15" actual/16" nominal depth. See Appendix E for standard shelving dimensions and capacity estimates.

Special education facilities serving students who cannot be mainstreamed, such as those with multiple handicaps (i.e., spina bifida, cerebral palsy, and learning disabilities) will require special provisions. Distance between shelving units, built-ins, and furniture will be greater to accommodate passage by handicapped students with special mobility needs. Height and depth of shelving will change in order to store kits and manipulatives and to accommodate physical access by students who have difficulty reaching and lifting.

All wall-attached and freestanding shelving in the media center must meet requirements as per bid specifications for adjustable shelving and shall be standard 3-foot lengths. Perimeter shelving should be used to the greatest extent possible in order to conserve floor space for furniture and program activities. Distance between freestanding shelving units and/or between shelving units and built-ins must be a minimum of 3'. In areas of high traffic volume, a minimum of 5' is required between rows of furniture and shelving. Freestanding shelving shall not exceed 15' in length and shall be placed as per working drawings.

Observation windows must begin a minimum of 45" from the floor to permit shelving beneath and should not interrupt 3-foot increments of continuous shelving of a specific height.

The reading and browsing areas will include a combination of wall-attached and freestanding shelving (1.3 linear feet per pupil is needed to meet the shelving requirements for books). The shelving will be standard adjustable library shelving to accommodate books and reference materials.

The standard perimeter shelving will be single-faced and wall-attached, with 10" actual/11" nominal depth.

Standard freestanding shelving units are to be double-faced, not more than 42" high, with a minimum of 10" actual/11" nominal depth. Freestanding units are not to exceed 15' in length. Reference shelving shall be 12" actual/13" nominal depth. Picture-book shelving shall be 12" actual/13" nominal depth with upright dividers.

Periodical shelving to accommodate display of current magazines will be a minimum of 45 linear feet, and will have sloped display shelves.

The office will have standard adjustable library shelving placed to accommodate books for a minimum of 45 linear feet. The shelving is to be single-faced, wall-attached, 12" actual/13" nominal depth.

The workroom, periodical storage room, professional library, and media production laboratory will have standard adjustable library shelving, 60+ linear feet, to accommodate materials to be processed. This wall-attached shelving is to be single-faced and adjustable, 15″ actual/16″ nominal depth, and in 3-foot standard sections.

The standard adjustable library shelving to accommodate professional books, periodicals, and audiovisual (AV) materials will allow for .25 linear feet per pupil. This wall-attached shelving is to be single-faced and adjustable, 15″ actual/16″ nominal depth, and in standard 3-foot sections.

AV storage requires heavy-duty, adjustable storage shelving 18″ deep, in 3-foot lengths, to be installed around the perimeter of the room for equipment. Four additional shelving units are to be installed in the center of the room.

Wet carrels. Wet, or wired, carrels are to be installed throughout the library media center. These may be single-faced, book stack hanging carrel units (see fig. 10) or freestanding units in a configuration determined by the individual architectural features of the room and as per working drawings.

Carrels should not have any shelves that will hinder the placement of a computer and a monitor in the unit, or deep sides, or high backs that hinder visual access by staff.

Each unit must have (or have access to) one or more 110-volt duplex outlets.

Display units. Any closed glass display cases will be freestanding and located inside the library media center. No glass display cabinets should be facing exterior walls. Exhibit cases will be freestanding units that match the furniture line and will be included in the furniture and shelving bid.

Wall surfaces. All wall surfaces should be of a tackable composition providing areas for borderless and unframed displays and assisting in sound absorption throughout the entire library media center. There will be no bordered bulletin board display areas.

Audiovisual screens. One 60″ × 60″ ceiling-mounted, electric projection screen with modular motor, low-voltage multiple switching, matte finish, and keystone elimination capacity is to be installed in the multipurpose area. Location must be

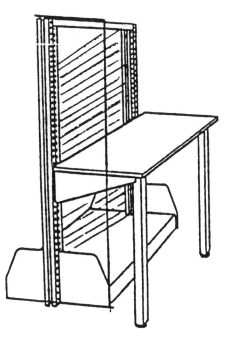

Fig. 10. Hanging-stack carrel unit

as per working drawings. Where ambient light will be a problem for front projection of audiovisual equipment, a plexiglass rearview screen with protective coating will be necessary.

Other Considerations

This section includes those items that do not fit in specific categories assigned by the format of the educational specifications, and those items that need repetition.

Access to mechanical rooms and air conditioning equipment serving the library media center complex should be from exterior corridors.

To provide good visibility and flexible room arrangement, the use of pillars or support posts in the library media center must be around the perimeter walls.

Sinks shall be at one end of built-in counters.

Special consideration should be given to electronic security in all areas of the library media center.

Extra security should be provided for the audiovisual equipment storage area.

Walls in the television studio, television distribution area, and audio studio should have special acoustical treatment to facilitate recording.

Special attention should be given to architectural features that promote the program and the facility to the entire school and community.

The educational specifications concludes with this section, which addresses the special needs of the program not included elsewhere in the document. The educational specifications document drives the design process, and its importance is evident throughout each phase of involvement of the architectural team. The architectural team's perspective is creative, sometimes abstract, and, at other times, linear and exact. An understanding of the perspective from which the architectural team operates will help the school team communicate effectively. When the role of each team is understood, the dialogue that is critical to a successful building program occurs on a solid footing. The architect's view is presented in chapter 3.

Reference

1. American Association of School Librarians and Association for Educational Communications and Technology, *Information Power: Guidelines for School Library Media Programs* (Chicago: American Library Association, 1988).

THREE

An Architect's View

Luther L. Eubanks

The design of a new or renovated school library media center can be an exciting experience. Even seasoned professionals, both in education and in the design professions, get caught up in the excitement of developing a fresh solution to a challenging problem. Every project offers a new series of design challenges and new possibilities for their solution. However, the design experience can be excruciatingly painful for the unprepared. That pain will last years beyond the design phase if the project is built from a poor design. Preparation of the education professional is critical to the evolution of a design that will serve the school community well.

The Design Team

The design team is typically thought of as the architect, along with staff and consultants, charged with the responsibility of producing a set of documents from which a building is built or remodeled. However, the "design team," in its broadest sense, must be viewed as all those involved in the process before ground-breaking ceremonies. There are actually two groups involved—the owner's group and the architect's group. For an outstanding result, both groups must be committed to the same goal.

The Owner

The owner's group includes the state department of education, the school district, the designated project manager for the owner, the school library media specialist, the school principal, other concerned staff, and parent participants. Private-school planning may include members of the school's governing board, founders, or benefactors in this team. Each member of the team will have a unique vision of what is required, what the facility is to accomplish, and how it should appear. Some, or all, of these participants may be involved in the actual design/review process. The owner's participants should be organized into a logical hierarchy with their respective duties and responsibilities defined. Good design is the result of respecting the diverse input on a project while avoiding "design by committee." A concise statement of all the owner's objectives and requirements is essential to the success of a project and should be incorporated into the educational specifications document.

The Architect

The consultant's or architect's group will generally include the architect, structural engineer, mechanical engineer, and electrical engineer. The architect will employ other consultants as may be needed, such as an interior designer, landscape architect, or civil engineer. In certain instances, the architect may elect to bring in highly specialized consultants, such as acoustical engineers or historical preservation specialists, to assist with very special conditions or concerns. The architect will assemble the professional team in response to the nature, size, and complexity of the problems to be solved.

Several staff members of the architectural firm will usually be involved in the project. The levels descend from principal (or partner) to project architect, to project manager, to draftsman. Shifts in key personnel directly associated with a project will usually occur as the work progresses through the various stages of the documents from design to construction. The larger the firm, the more specialized will be the roles of the individuals involved. School personnel must understand the architectural firm's internal organization, personnel, and procedures to make best use of the architect's services.

The Architect Selection Process

Selection of an architect or architectural firm for a particular project is a critical early step in the evolution of a design. Each school district or governing agency will have its own particular process for selecting professional design firms. Frequently, the architect is retained for a larger project of which the library media center is only one part. The relative importance of the library media center to the entire project must be evaluated before the selection process. The school library media specialist will be particularly sensitive to the program needs of library media services and may not be as concerned with other aspects of the project. It is the responsibility of the library media specialist to make these needs known and build a case for the unique characteristics and requirements of a superior library media center.

A detailed construction program that includes a statement of the problems to be solved and the educational specifications should be included in the "request for proposals" (RFP) sent out to selected design firms. The submittal requirements for responding to the RFP will vary depending on the selection process for the school district. Generally, the architect will submit a package containing the firm's standard 254 and 255 Forms with specified supplemental and visual data. The 254 Form is an American Institute of Architects (A. I. A.) document that describes the firm's staff, experience, and current work load. The 255 Form lists the firm's completed projects that are similar to the proposed

project. When a problem statement or program contains the words "new library media center" or "remodel library media center," most architects will realize they must address that issue in their initial submittals if they are to be considered for selection. If the firm has limited expertise in a particular facet of the problem, a consultant for that area will be listed in its 254. Once qualified to be among those selected to make a presentation, the architect will allot time to the library media center in proportion to its relative importance within the total project. The design firm selected should demonstrate the entire range of capabilities required to complete the project.

The Design Elements

Visual

Architecture relies on a complex interrelationship of individual components to create meaning. Just as individual letters are grouped into words, words into sentences, sentences into paragraphs, and so on to express meaning in language, components in architecture are assembled in a structured hierarchy to convey meaning. Complexity, style, and ambiguity exist in the various "symbols" of a building just as they do in writing. As in literature, the meaning of these symbols is influenced by relationship with one another, with other experiences, and with other buildings. Architects will frequently use such terms as *vocabulary, rhythm,* or *allusion* in describing their work.

Basic design elements—line, shape, form, color, texture, light, and shade—define every visible surface of the built environment. Surfaces frequently become the focus of architectural design because they can be depicted, visualized, and comprehended most readily. However, the most important aspect of architectural design is the resultant space defined, or at least suggested, by various surfaces. It is within this space that activities occur and from which the surrounding surfaces are viewed by the users.

Architectural spaces, in their most basic sense, may be thought of as "boxes"—boxes, both opened and closed, that contain people (students and staff), store things (materials and equipment), and facilitate events (program activities). Boxes the size of cabinets, the size of rooms, the size of buildings are organized to accomplish specific objectives. Even boxes that are not experienced directly have an impact through the resultant spaces created by their placement. An upper storage cabinet above a lower storage cabinet creates a "resultant space"—a work counter. Low bookshelves, a chair, and a plant or a change in ceiling height may define a special place for reading within a larger space. Two adjacent buildings and a wall may create a courtyard for special outdoor activities.

A distinction must be made between the nature of the surfaces and components of a building and the resultant spaces created by those surfaces and components. Regardless of the nature of the defining surfaces, the spaces created must be appropriate in size and scale to accommodate the intended activities.

Systems

Spaces are all, regardless of size and use, interrelated by systems that circulate vehicles, people, goods, electricity, electronic communications, conditioned air, water, and waste. Organization and management of these various circulation systems is critical, and examination and analysis of each system is an integral part of the design process. Some systems are unseen; their routing is an exercise in engineering and value analysis with implications being primarily initial cost, operating efficiency, and maintenance. Other systems, those which are visible, have both practical and aesthetic implications.

Circulation systems in architecture generally do not occur naturally. They are imposed by other design elements to control movement and activity. Systems that people experience directly should convey a sense of natural order that buildings or interiors respond to, rather than the reverse; the routing of vehicular and pedestrian traffic controls the sequence in which a series of spaces is encountered, how a building or a group of buildings is perceived from a particular vantage point, the types of noises that are generated, the pedestrian/vehicle conflicts that may occur, and the general sense of orientation or order that is conveyed.

Most people have had the experience of arriving at a strange place that at once seemed welcoming. They were certain they were in the right place and knew fairly well what to expect and where to go. Most people have also encountered sites and buildings that required a map and compass to navigate. Schools, which introduce new students and parents into their environs each year, need to establish this sense of naturally communicated order.

Physical Context

In architecture the visual aspects are dominant, but they are not the entire experience. The entire experience of the spaces people inhabit engages all the other senses as well. Added to the constructed environment, the elements of the natural environment—climate and geology—complete a rich palette of sensory stimulation.

Geographic and geologic features have an initial impact on the situation and orientation of any building. The physical impact of these features is most profound in the actual engineering of buildings, and is not generally something observable by the users. The relationship of a building to terrain, vegetation, the sun's path, and desirable views is an important part of the siting of a new building or the utilization of an existing one. The experience of how buildings look in their environment, inside and out, at different times of day or in various seasons of the year, is the subject of much study by architects, photographers, and artists. Those features are enduring and cannot be ignored, but their impact is subtle, generally predictable, and still primarily visual.

To all of the visual drama of the natural and constructed environment, add climatic conditions. It is climate that imposes the greatest impact, both visual and sensory, on the design of buildings. Buildings must be capable of maintaining appropriate conditions for the conduct of activities for which they were designed. Buildings, and all their support systems, must respond to the range of temperature, precipitation, prevailing winds, and relative humidity to which they and their inhabitants will be subjected. Climate has a profound effect on the structures that are built, the people who use them, and, in the case of school library media centers, the materials and systems used and stored throughout the interior.

Social Context

Buildings function within a social context just as they do within a physical context. The composition and individual elements of a design take on meaning based on past experiences with other buildings and on the education and the aspirations of both the architectural and school planning teams. For all of the real impact that the natural environment imposes on humans and the structures they build, the impact of intangible forces on design is probably more powerful, and less understood.

In virtually any metropolitan area of the world it is possible to see automobiles capable of speeds over one hundred miles per hour, equipped with front air dams and rear deck spoilers that enhance handling by imposing the proper aerodynamic forces. On the same street may be found a four-wheel-drive vehicle with the amazing off-road capability to scale treacherous mountain roads or trails in all kinds of weather. Both vehicles are probably hundreds of miles from the nearest raceway or mountain, sitting in bumper-to-bumper traffic, transporting owners who are neither racers nor mountaineers. The intangible forces of society—imagination, fantasy, desire—and of Madison Avenue are very real indeed.

The same social and economic forces influence the design of buildings. Tourists and corporate travelers can circle the globe and experience buildings that are, with the exception of the view outside, virtually indistinguishable from one another in terms of building technology and aesthetic form and expression. People today expect to encounter a similar level of comfort within buildings regardless of locale or climate. They generally do not question whether the building is environmentally appropriate and energy efficient any more than whether their wardrobe or vehicle is suited to visit both Connecticut and Arizona in the same month. Their primary focus is on social rather than climatic suitability. The distinctions that should be obvious are that wardrobes and automobiles are not anchored to a specific piece of ground with a specific climate and geography for their entire usable life and that the life spans of these "constructed environments" are vastly different.

Although the technical engineering and construction expertise exist to make inappropriate buildings habitable under a wide range of climatic conditions by using artificial conditioning systems, there is a penalty to pay. When excessive performance capabilities are expanded to the scale of a building, the consequences are much more severe with regard to the long-term costs, especially in terms of energy consumption.

The Result

There are many examples of functionally well-conceived buildings that fulfill their programmatic requirements and yet ignore an area's indigenous architecture. This immediately deprives users of potentially valuable experiences and may eventually desensitize them to those experiences. Aside from buildings that convey no sense of place, there is left behind a legacy of inefficient buildings, overly reliant on the consumption of electricity and fossil fuels. Such buildings convey an enduring message about how people choose to live with and experience their environment.

Limited budgets and rising construction costs make it simpler to focus on the readily quantifiable—how much space at what cost. All other considerations

become secondary, at best. Every component of the building must be evaluated in terms of its cost and contribution to the overall project. Designs should evolve out of exploration of various ways to solve the same problem. Seek out the "twofers." Twofers are those features of a design that give you two for the price of one. For example, a huge arched window on the north side of a reading room can be a focal point from the inside as well as the outside. Given sufficient ceiling height, it can illuminate the reading areas by day and be a beacon to the community by night. This feature must be considered from many aspects, including energy, aesthetics, security, and initial costs. If this solution is compared to a series of small windows with the same total combined area, it may not be any more costly and the result may be infinitely more effective and memorable.

Exterior areas surrounding the school library media center provide opportunities for dual benefit. Simple patio and landscape spaces make for attractive views from within the building and usable spaces for special activities. In northern climates, these may need to be compact spaces situated on the sunny, south face of the building and protected from the wind. In sunny, arid climates, morning and afternoon spaces may develop on opposite sides of the building in the open shade cast by the building. When covered walkway connectors are used, an expansion in width and height of a section can produce an outdoor room for a minimum of additional expenditure. If this wide overhang is situated to control sunlight and glare within the building, there is an added benefit.

Good architecture must strive to strike a balance among the diverse requirements of aesthetic, social, economic, and technical considerations. The quality and effectiveness of a particular design are not so much related to the budget available but to the depth of understanding of and willingness to deal with the problems at hand. Instead of trying to defeat or ignore nature and society, architecture should work with and embrace them to achieve a certain harmony conducive to a specific geographic and climatic environment.

The advent of the electronic age, which depends so much on artificial climate control for the protection of sensitive electronic equipment, has led to a dramatic expansion of human visual experience with possibly a decrease in stimulation of the other senses. There exists a wealth of sensitive architecture in every part of the country that is responsive on both environmental and social levels. Architects and owners should not succumb to the current fad or fashion in architecture. To do so deprives the users of a vital part of the experience of the natural environment and cultural heritage. It is not necessary to draw inspiration for designs from the pages of international architectural publications. Schools, in particular, should be places where children not only study complex relationships but can experience, be stimulated, and be educated by them as well.

The Design Process

The architectural design process occurs in several different phases, each becoming progressively more refined and detailed as ideas are developed and more of the architect's team become involved. The phases are generally classified as (1) conceptual, (2) schematic, (3) design development, and (4) construction documents (working drawings and specifications).

The exact nomenclature, the nature of the work to be performed, and specific services excluded in each phase are described in detail in the contract for professional services. Specific types of submittals and submittal dates may also be included in the agreement. School systems often have specialized staff and thorough procedures in place to deal with this part of the development process.

The entire school team, whether involved in the negotiation of the architect's contract or not, should have some understanding of the services and critical dates in each phase of the project. This ensures input is given to the architectural team at appropriate times. If library media professionals are not in a position to deal directly with the architect, then additional time and effort are required to express their views through other parties or documents. This becomes even more of a challenge. A critical requirement or worthwhile idea that is overlooked early in the design can be difficult and expensive to incorporate later.

The architect will spend a great deal of time in problem solving—making sure the *school's* problems are solved. The architects, by training and innate talents, work in general abstract terms to resolve problems that are concrete and specific. Without sufficient explanation, the architect may oversimplify a problem or concentrate on the artistic or aesthetic aspects. Problem-solving capabilities, three-dimensional visualization, and artistic sensitivity are among the architect's talents brought to bear on a project. Management of these talents and, therefore, the direction of the project are influenced greatly by the owner. The school team must not be

left out of the decision-making process. The educational specifications for the library media center facility must be clearly communicated by those who best understand its complex program elements—the library media professionals.

Programming and Feasibility

Specific critical activities precede the actual design process. Predesign activities are generally referred to as *programming* and *feasibility*. The programming phase attempts to quantify the types and sizes of spaces required for the particular project; the feasibility study examines what will be required to translate that program into the reality of a building.

The educational specifications include general information about the purpose of the building, users to be accommodated, descriptions of the activities, interrelationship of interior spaces, net square footage requirements, hours of operation, and other requirements. More detailed technical requirements, such as performance specifications, lighting levels and controls, electrical power requirements for equipment, furniture and fixture requirements, and certain finish materials, should also be included. A good educational specifications document provides a statement of all the objectives of the finished facility, focusing on what it is supposed to do and what considerations should be made for various activities. The educational specifications, however, should avoid describing how construction should be done or exactly what the facility should look like.

The feasibility study examines site acquisition or additional development, utility service, pertinent governmental regulations, gross square footage of construction, associated fees, and other possible requirements to translate the preliminary program into more specific recommendations, cost estimates, and methods of financing or funding. Feasibility includes not only the initial costs associated with building or remodeling but also the costs of financing and operating the facility over time. The study may also investigate similar buildings in terms of amenities provided and attendant expenses to verify the ratio of costs versus benefits.

The architect may or may not be involved in either the programming or the feasibility process. Sometimes this initial work is done by school staff, district specialists, outside consultants, other architects, or any number of possible combinations. It is important to have qualified professional design and construction assistance during this phase if the written program is to be realistic in terms of specific requirements and costs. Many projects would be better served by engaging the architect earlier in the process in order to have assistance in identifying overall program weaknesses or oversights and explaining possibilities and limitations as a result of specific observations or investigations into the project and site.

Meetings

Whenever possible, direct contact during the design stage between the individuals in the architect's organization and the owner's representatives is preferred. The attendance of a firm's principal at meetings without key design staff members is influenced greatly by the practices peculiar to specific regions of the country, the attitude of the architectural firm, the composition of the design team, and the nature of the specific project.

Few contemporary architects, or principals of the firm, except in small practices, can be financial managers, designers, marketing directors, technical experts, production supervisors, and construction managers all at the same time. Attendance at meetings by principals of the architectural firm who are not directly involved in the design process can result in nuances of meaning and intent being lost. This can result in missed opportunities for creative and constructive exchanges of ideas leading to superior solutions.

When the time comes for a major presentation, the principal-in-charge or project architect will certainly participate. The review and presentation process should be structured to make best use of the time of the school district personnel as well as the architect. A good principal of a firm will be involved in the development and review of ideas within the firm's organization, providing the benefit of experience even if not attending all meetings.

Schematic Design

The first step in the schematic design process is review and evaluation of the school team's program document for the entire construction project and the educational specifications. Setting priorities for the major design considerations and structuring, in a physical sense, begins here. A hierarchy of spaces is established and forms the framework for the organization of progressively smaller components. The objective of this phase is to identify and locate the major components and subcomponents of a comprehensive whole that works at all levels or scales of operation.

Establishment of a common nomenclature based on prior documents and shared experiences can be of great benefit and help to avoid misunderstandings in interpreting the written words of educational specifications. School visits, slide shows, and a review of plans for existing facilities are excellent ways to facilitate understanding and exchanges of information and philosophies. This learning experience can be greatly improved when it is reinforced with examples of diagrams and plans the architect has used to express abstract ideas as the design developed.

Just as the school library media specialist today has responsibility for coordinating a wide range of complex services and equipment, the architect has responsibility for the direction of all of the professionals involved on the architectural team, and eventually for limited supervision of the general contractor during the construction process. Most architects can readily relate to the rapid change in both the library media and architectural professions and the impact that the computer and the information age are having on the way work is performed. The nature of an architect's own work facilitates understanding of the activities performed in a typical school library media center, because the school library media specialist and architect share many of the same problems in the storage and retrieval of diverse types of materials.

Because of their training and basic thought process, most architects attempt to translate everything into graphic form, appropriate or not, to substantiate what is sometimes a mostly intuitive process. The architect will translate the written educational specifications into diagrams to demonstrate the interrelationship of all the various project components. The bubble diagrams found in the educational specifications document are also employed in this process. Certain issues are actually easier to visualize and discuss in this simplified form because too much information tends to cloud large-scale issues. The different areas described in the educational specifications as a whole are now translated into the architect's diagrams, which resemble floor plans for the entire school facility construction project. Other visualization tools employed by the architect include circulation diagrams or adjacency matrices. Color depicting usage patterns and arrows indicating circulation flow are tools frequently used by architects to express different possibilities for how a program might translate itself.

The largest scale at which the program components will be viewed is at the site level. This site may be a freestanding parcel of land, a portion of a campus, or a segment of a larger building. At this level such issues as relationship to site features and other buildings or functions, proximity to classrooms, access to parking, and aesthetic orientation will be assessed. There may be off-site considerations, such as views, hazards, or distractions, that could also have bearing on the design of the building.

The next scale of evaluation is at the level of the individual building. Here each primary component is looked at as it relates to other primary components, and to the key issues identified for the site. Logical access points related to circulation patterns, location and orientation for natural lighting or views, access to and location of utility spaces and delivery areas, and other issues affecting the building/site interface are studied.

Finally, individual rooms and spaces are evaluated in terms of their location within the building. Traffic paths, zoning of quiet and noisy areas, visual control, and other functional relationships are explored.

The most effective or most promising of these schematic drawings are then developed into rough scale drawings. These translate into graphic diagrams with proportions and scale dimensions relating to actual shapes and sizes of a required space. These drawings will generally begin with two-dimensional site plans and floor plans, and then progress into sections and elevations. As the design develops, the dimensional plans express the vertical dimension.

At this point in the process it is essential to compare the written educational specifications with the design sketches under development. The school planning team should check to be certain that all spaces, sizes, relationships, and requirements are being addressed. Design is not a straight-line progression from written word to finished building. The purpose of the schematic design phase is to explore on paper how an imagined building and all of its components will function. This is the time when the experience of the school staff needs to be drawn upon in the evaluation of design and design alternatives. All school representatives should be sensitive to their own experiences as well as the experience and reputation of the architectural design team. Conflicts will be pointed out and arrival at solutions or compromises will be necessary. There will almost always be minor deviations, and occasionally major departures, from a given program statement as a result of discoveries made in design and analysis. Documentation, in writing, should delineate the changes and the reason for the changes as they occur.

Design Development

Once the program components have evolved into the basic framework and geometry of a building plan, it is time to integrate the technical planning for the systems that will be required. Structural systems must be evaluated and component sizes estimated. Mechanical and electrical systems must be reviewed to verify if initial assumptions for room sizes, locations, and routing are adequate. Lighting schemes and a reflected ceiling plan start to emerge.

At this point in the process, as engineers start to participate actively in the design and as more individuals become involved, costs increase. The architect switches from exploring the possibilities of design to planning and directing the efforts of various groups to accomplish the mission. Changes become increasingly more difficult and costly to make. Deadlines and schedules must be examined and committed to by all parties. The architect/owner relationship sometimes becomes more businesslike and less personal.

Input from the owner now is limited to choices within a fairly narrow band. Even though this is a period of technical or engineering activity similar to the architect's schematic design phase, it is often too late to introduce additional technical requirements. The implications of technical considerations on the design are discussed only to the extent that they affect the accomplishment of the approved schematic design.

Construction Documents

The designs and drawings to this point, whether conceptual, schematic, or design development, are referred to collectively as "preliminary." Upon approval of the preliminary drawings, the architect and engineers begin preparing working drawings and specifications from which the building and all of its components will be constructed.

The working drawings, variously referred to as sets of plans, prints, or blueprints, are prepared by the architect and engineers. These drawings contain all of the basic graphic, notational, and dimensional data required to describe to a general contractor and subcontractors the nature and scope of the work to be performed. Written specifications generally accompany the drawings and describe in detail the standards of construction practice, the materials to be used, and procedures for construction of all of the various items shown on the plans. These specifications also cover general requirements of the contract. Together the plans and specifications form the legal basis of the contract for construction of the project.

The architect should explain the sheet organization and symbol reference system used in the drawings. If unfamiliar with reading plans and placed in a position of dealing directly with some aspect of the development of drawings for a project, the school staff should have the architect recommend books or local programs that cover these skills. The school representatives must learn to read the drawings, use a scale, and ask questions.

The school staff should review final plans carefully to detect any oversights or misunderstandings on the part of the architect. It is especially important that the final plans be checked, just as the early schematic drawings, for compliance with the educational specifications or the adjusted construction program. This time it is critical to check for details that may have been overlooked or were previously under development. In addition, the front end of the specifications will contain important general information relating to the roles and duties of the architect, owner, and contractor.

Since most school projects are public, they are subject to competitive bidding. The project is advertised for bid according to the institution's requirements, and the construction documents are obtained by interested, qualified general contractors. Prior to a specified number of days before the bids are due, changes can usually be made by means of an "addendum." If a mistake or omission is discovered, adding the necessary correction or information is relatively simple, and the construction cost will still reflect a fair market value as a result of the competitive environment of bidding. Once the award of a bid or contract is made, changes must be introduced by means of a change order, which generally adds to the cost. Architects dread the paperwork, owners hate to see their contingency funds reduced, and contractors love to get a chance to tack a healthy profit onto this additional work. The contractor knows that even if a change order is costly, the cost will be even greater to correct by remodeling after the building is completed. Corrections are less costly when made before construction has commenced.

Budgets

Predetermined staged or phased construction and additive alternates are the only ways to control costs once committed to a specific building program. Phased construction anticipates future building or improvements as a part of an overall plan. Additive alternates, identified as elements desirable but not essential to the program, are bid with the base building allowing the owner to coast up to the budget without running past it. This enables the owner to select the highest priority alternates that will stay within the budget, or to identify the additional funds required to build the alternates at the same time as the base bid construction. Controlling project costs is critical, and the best method is through a fine-tuned educational specifications document.

Conclusion

The design professional is an essential member of the total design team. The architect by training and experience can assist in the transformation of a written statement of needs into a completed facility that accommodates all of the various activities contemplated by that statement. The architect is, however, only a member of the team. No individual is more knowledgeable about the requirements of a specific school library media center than the school library media specialist responsible for that facility. That depth of knowledge must be used from the early design and predesign stages to ensure the maximum result from the collective efforts of all involved in the design and construction process. The school library media specialist must strive to communicate ideas to the architect in terms that can be understood just as the architect must strive to understand, interpret, and clarify information and needs expressed by the library media specialist and others involved in the process.

Much thought and care must be given to the written educational specifications, the selection of the architect, and the design process. A well thought-out educational specifications document, a cooperative design team, and open channels of communication will produce a school library media center to serve the school community well in the years ahead.

FOUR

Renovation of a School Library: A Case Study

Nancy Bard and Pam Spencer

Rationale for Renovation

One of twenty-three high schools of the Fairfax County, Virginia, school district, Thomas Jefferson was built in 1962. In 1984, after twenty-three years of continual use, the high school was being considered for closing because of declining enrollment. At the same time, plans for a magnet high school program with emphasis on science and technology were being studied. The decision was made to house the program in the Thomas Jefferson High School, which would become the Thomas Jefferson High School for Science and Technology. In the fall of 1985, two distinct schools began to coexist in the building. Each succeeding year, a class of Thomas Jefferson students was assimilated into a nearby high school and another class was added to the magnet school's science and technology program. This arrangement continued until the fall of 1987, when the building was occupied solely by freshmen, sophomores, and juniors enrolled in the science and technology magnet program.

When we entered as school library media specialists in the fall of 1987, the building plant of Thomas Jefferson was typical of those built in the 1960s. The exterior walls of the library media center were covered with aqua tiles. The interior housed tall shelving. There were high ceilings, linoleum floors,

old venetian blinds, and poor lighting. The school had been built when library media centers predominantly housed book collections and, consequently, had limited audiovisual equipment and storage space. Over the years the addition of newer technology, such as microfiche readers and reader-printers, contributed to increasingly cramped, disorganized spaces that did little to facilitate maximum use of the resources. The need for a seven million dollar renovation of the school, with the library media center among the first areas to be revitalized, was evident.

As practicing school library media specialists who knew little about the planning and process of renovating a school, we searched for guidelines in the district. No written guidelines were to be found among the resources available, and it was determined that a case study of such a project would be helpful to other library media specialists who might be confronted by similar circumstances.

The Planning Process

Producing a design or layout for the library media center needs to be a cooperative effort among the personnel involved in the project—specifically the school administrator, library media specialists, school staff, and the architectural firm. This process is one of the most important aspects of the renovation. Because each situation is unique, the planning timetable will vary. The first meeting will probably occur one to two years before the actual construction begins. Subsequent sessions and discussions will occur during the planning stages.

Design Revisions

Because planning began before school library media specialists were employed for the magnet school program, the district supervisor provided preliminary input during the first planning phases, and the design phase of the library facility had been completed. Subsequent consultation with the architect provided some opportunity to incorporate features we felt were desirable or essential. Blueprints had already been drawn, but suggested changes in the furniture and shelving layout and some new display features were added to the existing plans.

After examining the shelving and furniture layout, we suggested freestanding bookshelves arranged diagonally to replace the fingerlike extensions of high shelves perpendicular to the back wall as designed by the architect. It was agreed that this arrangement would create an open, expansive atmosphere in the main reading room that would welcome students and facilitate supervision by the library media center staff. The expansion of the facility to include storage and technology rooms would alleviate the cramping caused by inadequate facilities. The floor plan, incorporating these changes, is shown in figure 11.

The district library media supervisor and the architect assisted in checking the drawings for adequate electrical outlets, light switches, access doors, and storage spaces in all areas of the library media center. This consultation was invaluable. During this process, the omission of a door between the online reference and the periodical storage rooms was discovered, a mistake that would have cost the staff many unnecessary steps when retrieving periodicals. It was also noticed that there were no electrical outlets along any of the walls in the online reference room. Two power poles, located in the center of the room, were the only source of electricity, and were inadequate to support the requirements of the computers that would be housed in that room. Such cross-checks and consultation were key to rectifying mistakes and catching omissions.

Design Additions

The next task was to make additions to the design drawings. Lack of available wall space for display of student work around the main reading room was a problem. There were several solutions, but we were not sure how they could be developed. One idea was to have display areas in the library media center to showcase student projects and exhibits. The architects offered a unique design of open niches that could be lighted and would be deep and wide enough to house displays. These would be located in a bulkhead spanning the width of the library media center. This bulkhead design, with an arch over the circulation desk, resulted in one of the most outstanding architectural features of the library media center (fig. 12). The design complements the main entrance to the school.

There was also need for a large showcase in the outside entryway, which, as it was designed, offered little to attract patrons as they approached. A large, lighted showcase was added to the drawings to eliminate this deficiency, but the architects failed to include shelves or wall-backing material in the design. These items were added to make the showcase usable.

Because the school emphasizes science and technology, we wanted to incorporate this theme into the center's design. The architects were asked to include an aquarium in the library media center, and this request was translated into a custom-built circulation desk housing a specially built aquarium. A 150-gallon tank is situated at the far end of the circulation desk, where the swimming fish attract the interest of students and visitors.[1]

The funds available for renovation had influenced decision making. A larger facility, one that would include a multipurpose room, was needed, but there was not enough funding to allow such expansion. Standard items for any new school, such as air conditioning, carpeting, lighting, dropped ceilings, and window miniblinds, would be part of the renovation budget. Since additional square footage was financially impossible, the goal would be to make the space that was available more usable and workable.

Preparing for Transition

Finding Temporary Housing

Two months before the anticipated moving date, school administrators notified the library media staff that it was necessary to find an alternative location for the center. A space was needed that would provide access both to materials and to some program activities. The staff was unable to locate space in the existing school facility that would house the

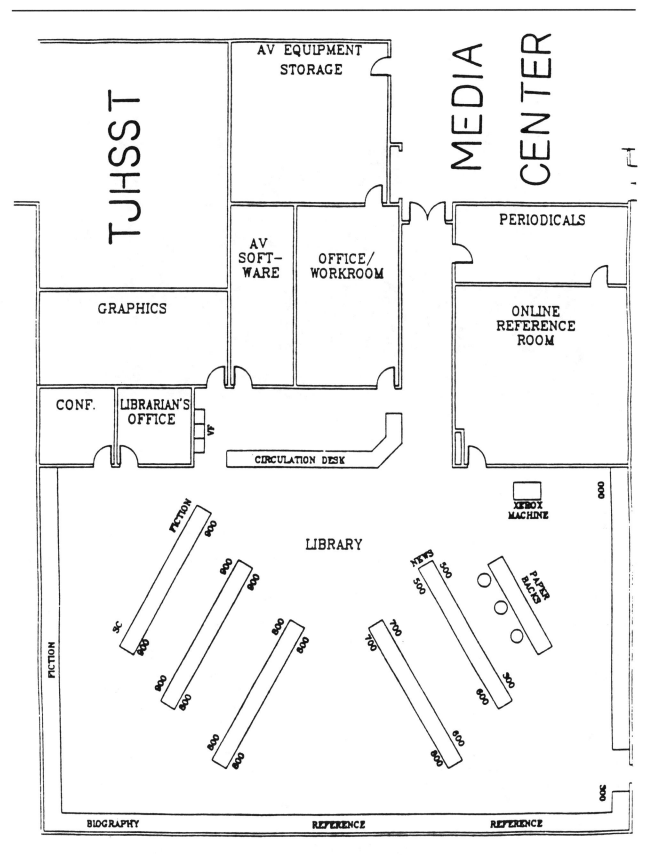

Fig. 11. Library media center floor plan. Thomas Jefferson High School for Science and Technology, Fairfax County, Va.

Fig. 12.   Bulkhead design with art and circulation desk in renovated library media center.

entire collection and support a total program. Most of the book and audiovisual collection would have to be packed for storage. The search began for space that would allow provision of the best possible service to students and teachers and house a small reference and a circulating paperback collection.

The final choice for location of the temporary library media center was also contingent on the space available to house those pieces of equipment vital to minimal service. The following equipment, identified as essential, provided guidelines for selection of temporary space: coin-operated copy machine, card catalog and shelflist, laminating machine, newspapers on microfilm, microfilm reader and reader-printer, computer, circulating paperback collection, circulating reference collection, and vertical file cabinets.

Several locations were considered, including a robotics lab, a loggia area, temporary classroom buildings outside the school, a two-room faculty workroom, and an upstairs classroom. The classroom was chosen because it offered storage facilities across the hall.

The closed-circuit television/cable system and the book detection system had to be disengaged and stored to prevent damage from the dirt and dust of renovation. Enough lead time was planned for personnel to accomplish this task.

Classroom Collections

While preparation for the move continued, plans were made to meet the diverse needs and interests of students and faculty while the main facility was unusable. Teachers were alerted that the entire collection would not be available for several months. Teachers who needed materials had two options: to provide a classroom reserve collection that would be kept until the new facility was ready, or to prepare a book cart of reserve books to be used for various study units.

The faculty assisted in identifying materials needed for assignments and projects. All items for classroom collections and book carts were entered on computer lists and were given to the teachers, who assumed responsibility for circulation and return of the items upon completion of the renovation. Books returned before the library media center reopened would be packed in boxes, labeled, and sent to storage.

Weeding

The prospect of a new library media center was the perfect time to purge the collection of books and audiovisual materials that were no longer applicable to the curriculum or that contained outdated information. Even though the collection had been weeded several years earlier in preparation for its new science-technology emphasis, additional weeding was necessary to prevent packing, storing, and unpacking materials that should have been eliminated. Titles that were still useful but in poor condition were considered for replacement. In many cases old hardcover titles were supplanted by paperbacks or reinforced paperbacks at reasonable prices. Videotapes replaced faded slides and filmstrips.

Several library media specialists who had attended an American Association of School Librarians (AASL) workshop on weeding assisted in evaluating the materials.[2] They devised a chart that contains criteria for removal of titles from the collection.

Packing and Storing the Collection

Students were allowed maximum use of the collection until the materials had to be packed. A month had been allocated for packing, but the process was not as time consuming as was originally thought; it could have been completed easily in seven to ten working days. Volunteers assisted with this process. Since this procedure is physically taxing, two-person teams were set up, with one person assembling and taping the flat boxes and the other removing books from the shelves and packing them in order in the box. The packing process was planned in advance and boxes were ordered to contain a collection of approximately 14,000 books, five-year backfiles for 125 magazine subscriptions, audiovisual software, and supplies. Approximately 700 boxes were used.

Uniformity in strength and size of the boxes was necessary. The boxes, measuring 19" × 11" × 13" with a strength of 200 pounds per square inch, were deep enough to contain oversized audiovisual software boxes and art books, or a number of books, without becoming too heavy or unwieldy.[3] Handheld tape dispensers for 2-inch-wide strapping tape were purchased to ease assembly of these boxes. Approximately 16 rolls of tape were used. Boxes used for the library media center could be broken down and recycled for additional moves by school staff during renovation.

A general marking system was used to label boxes. Broad Dewey categories, such as 000, 100, 200, and biography, were used. The boxes were labeled in shelf order within each category, for example, "200/Box #1." Also indicated on each box

was the location to which it should be delivered in the renovated facility, for example, "400/Box #1/ Reference Room."

Once the boxes were filled, custodians helped move them to the designated storage area. In order to remain in control of the collection and reduce the risk of loss, we had to find a single storage area in the school large enough to hold all the materials. Faculty members inevitably asked for specific books after the collection was packed and stored. Taking faculty members to the storage area to observe the stacks of boxes helped them understand that, once boxed, the items were not retrievable.

Materials returned after the initial packing had taken place were labeled "miscellaneous." This label alerted staff of the need for sorting when these boxes were shipped to the renovated library media center. The same was true for magazine subscriptions; after being checked in, they were stored with the boxes of books and supplies.

Locating storage space for the equipment was also a problem. A large vault housed videotape players. Other audiovisual items, such as overhead, movie, and slide projectors, were checked out to teachers for the school year. During the summer months, all audiovisual equipment was locked in two classrooms where it was easily accessible for maintenance and repair. The computer was moved to the temporary library.

Furniture storage was a major problem because of the space required for such large pieces. The furniture was stacked in unused parts of stairways and hallways, rather than at a remote storage facility, thus preventing possible damage and loss during moving.

Temporary Facilities

It was difficult to identify the temporary classroom as a library media center. A sign, "Yes, honest, this is the library media center," was placed outside the classroom to encourage students to enter. The facility was cramped, noisy, and hot, but the staff was able to function. A small storeroom across the hall provided space to shelve a sizable reference collection and a partial audiovisual collection. All the items identified as necessary were housed, but most of the television and video units had to be stored on another floor. The temporary library media center became quite crowded by the end of summer with many boxes of new and returned books and new equipment.

Service to students and faculty was minimal during the eight months in temporary facilities. Students and staff could check out new periodicals only, some fiction paperbacks, and the reference books that were in the "branch library" across the hall. Orders for books and films continued, the card catalog was put in order, and the few materials that were accessible circulated. Severely reduced quarters limited the program and placed great strain on staff, but we were able to watch and chart the progress of the demolition and renovation. Slides of the entire process have been incorporated into freshman library orientations, giving students and staff a greater appreciation of the renovated library media center facility as well as its programs and services.

Murphy's Law: Moving to the New Facility

Once the renovation of the library media center was completed, planning was necessary to reduce problems encountered during the move and to reduce further strain on staff and program. The need for additional classrooms and storage space while other areas of the school were being renovated meant moving into the library media center before the heat could be turned on, and before windows and shelving were installed. It was difficult to estimate an opening time because even the contractors didn't know when the facility would pass county inspection. The delivery of 700 boxes of library materials with no shelving to house them further complicated the process. Students assisted in organizing the boxes into call number order in the anticipated shelf location. Flexibility became the operational guideline.

Further complications occurred when the company hired to build the shelving went bankrupt, and the contractor had to bid on the shelving at court auction. While waiting for the custom shelving to be completed, we organized the offices and magazine room, stored supplies, assembled some of the AV carts, installed computers, and completed some of the daily tasks of film and book ordering. As shelving was installed, the collection was put in place.

Reshelving the collection took much longer than packing it. Because the boxes were packed in call number order, some volunteers preferred to unpack and shelve directly from the boxes. Others preferred to unpack to a book cart, check the order of the books, and then place them on the shelves.

During the move-in, the library media center was never closed, although it was unusable for large-group research for approximately eight months. Paperbacks were housed in the entrance area, the copy machine was operational, and, when there was enough space for the furniture, students were allowed to study wherever a spot was available. Once everything was in place, the instructional program was reactivated and orientation was provided to familiarize students with the new arrangement.

New Services in the New Facility

The custom circulation desk was designed by the architects to accommodate the proposed automated circulation system and the online public access catalog. It was built to house a computer, printer, and a file server. The computer screen needed to be at least twelve feet away from the security system to avoid interference from the security detection system.

The online reference room was a brand new concept—there had been no computer services in the former facility. The room was built to house three computer stations dedicated to online retrieval of information from remote databases and four stations utilizing CD-ROM equipment. This room also houses the microfiche collection, microfiche readers, reader-printer, periodical indexes, and special collections of current reprints of articles.

A graphics laboratory was incorporated into the library media center design. A laminating machine, a copy stand and camera, a computer, and a laser printer were all included in this area. The room also has a sink, ample cabinets, and counter space. Strips of electrical outlets were installed on both sides of the room, providing adequate electricity to operate production equipment. Three other new areas were included in the renovation: a periodical storage room with deep, built-in shelves; an audiovisual storage area with similar built-in shelving; and an audiovisual equipment room with large shelves, a work bench, and an area designated for the television head-end equipment. Storage was provided in three additional rooms.

The furniture budget was limited because much of the equipment allocation was spent on computers and hardware for the automated circulation system. Some new items were purchased: an index table for the periodical indexes, a newspaper rack, and office desks and chairs. The original library media center tables and chairs are still being used, and blend well with the new surroundings.

The renovation process was a tedious and sometimes frustrating experience. But the renovated facility produced a beautiful, functional library media center—a showplace for this school of science and technology. The process of renovation, even though planned, unavoidably reduced the program and placed great strain on staff. Today, however, the facility will support the students, teachers, and library media specialists as we move the science and technology program at Thomas Jefferson High School into the next century.

References

1. The incorporation of a fish tank containing water under pressure close to computer equipment and file servers as a method of marketing the program could have been avoided if the planning process were not a modification of what has been included in the first three chapters of this book. This design feature could be a disaster waiting to happen and would not have been a late inclusion in the planning process had marketing the program been articulated in the educational specifications document. This obviously was an afterthought in the design.

2. Dorothy Liegl, *"Weeding the Collection"* (Presentation at the Fourth National Conference of the American Association of School Librarians, Minneapolis, September 25, 1986).

3. Movement of loaded cartons is often a contractual or negotiated item. The school district's contract with custodial and/or maintenance personnel should be checked to ensure that carton size and weight are within acceptable limits.

FIVE

From Renovation to
New Construction: A Case Study

Renovation of an older school building presents unique problems. Load-bearing walls, existing plumbing and electrical conduits, the expanded use of the site subsequent to original construction, and evidence of asbestos in the original building are all factors that affect the planning process. These factors also make the renovation and expansion process different from that of a project involving new construction.

Rationale

Markham Elementary School in Pompano Beach, Florida, was originally constructed in 1967. Its enrollment has increased in size each year, from 552 in 1985 to 685 in 1989. The school serves a minority student population of African Americans (92%). Within its geographic boundaries are a major interstate highway, a railway, light industrial complexes, many warehouses, and a farmers' market. The area contains dilapidated housing projects as well as a community of duplexes and some small, single-family dwellings. It is also a neighborhood of long tradition—an area in which children of farmhands grew, were educated, and became successful. The school's neighborhood is part of a larger community extending to choice properties that house an older,

very affluent population along the Atlantic Ocean. The leaders in the school community and those of the more affluent sections of the city joined to express the need for renovation of an aging, overcrowded, and underequipped school structure.

In 1987, a major bond issue was promoted in the Broward County school system, the result of a state department of education survey of all facilities in the district and a district assessment that some facilities were substandard and could not meet current program needs. The survey identified individual schools' needs for expansion and renovation, as well as the need for new buildings to meet a steadily increasing enrollment. The bond issue program was responsive to individual school requests and resulted in 40 schools planning new library media centers and another 58 schools expanding and renovating their library media centers. There would also be 27 new schools built within seven years.

The success of the bond issue provided capital project funds to begin the district's massive construction program. A construction program of the magnitude of the Broward County School District presents unique problems and solutions. The district's countywide curriculum, minimum performance standards, and great mobility within the system of both students and staff make continuity and minimum standards for all schools necessary. The Markham Elementary School construction, as well as that for all schools in the district, would meet *district* educational specifications.

The Planning Process

The library media center educational specifications were developed for each level—elementary, middle, and high school—by a committee of practitioners working with the district director of the library media program. The written specifications resulted from a study of the professional literature, visits to schools, examination of manufacturers' products, discussions with architects and engineers, and brainstorming sessions by practitioners. Once accepted by the committee, the educational specifications had to be approved by the district administration and then by the governing officials—the school board.

The construction program for Markham Elementary School included a new administration area, additional classrooms, and the conversion of seven rooms to accommodate expansion of the library media center. The educational specifications would provide the guide for renovation of a facility built in the sixties—single story with the library media center in a central location but contained by adjoining classroom spaces at either end and by corridors along the sides (see fig. 13). There were no windows to provide natural light and ventilation. The entire plant had few windows, reducing perceived security risks and distractions to students.

Examination of the size of the property, the existing spaces, and the scope of the renovation program indicated that the new administrative area would require an addition to the front of the building that would alter the architectural design. The existing library media center was located in a core area; its expansion would replace classrooms and expand the center to an exterior wall, but still would not meet the standards. Both of these renovations would not be cost-effective. Plans to request additional funding were made.

In the meantime, other areas of the building were to be recarpeted immediately. During the recarpeting, it was discovered that the building had been contaminated by asbestos. A simple procedure became a major obstacle not only for the recarpeting but for all further work; renovation schedules had to be replaced by asbestos abatement plans. As unfortunate as this was, it redirected the thinking, particularly as it related to the library media center.

Asbestos abatement provided additional funds and made it possible to provide a new library media center and expand the administration complex into the area formerly assigned to the library media center. It was cost-effective to plan a new library media center facility that would meet the standards of the district's educational specifications for new schools. The decision was made to build an entirely new library media center in a separate building.

The available land for a new library media center building was limited. The school planning team, the project manager, and the architectural firm were all anxious to locate the center as close to classrooms as possible; to provide accessibility during hours when the school might not be open and on off-calendar days; and to make the library media center distinctive and easily recognizable to the educational community and the political-geographical community the school serves. The availability of land required placement of the library media center at the back of the campus but in an area visible from the street (see fig. 14). The center could be accessed from a parking lot area using a paved walkway. Covered walkways would connect all other areas of the campus with the library media center.

Schematic Design

Having determined placement of the building, the next task was to examine the educational specifications with the architectural team. Dialogue during this process allowed the school team to respond to questions from the architects regarding program and function of spaces. The bubble diagram (see fig. 15) showed adjacencies and spatial relationships, and provided the basis for discussion. The spaces depicted in figure 15 are not identical to those in the model educational specifications, reflecting local practices and procedures for development of the district's document.

There was still confusion regarding the use of the spaces, and it was clear that school visits would be critical to the architect's understanding of the concepts. Arrangements were made for visits to schools with model programs. The architect spent several mornings observing good library media programs in operation. During these visits, the school planning team explained the activities and related them to the bubble diagram, the explanation of the program functions found in the educational specifications, and the facilities list. This exercise provided a base for the architect's conceptualization.

Numerous meetings between the architect and the school planning team followed. The dialogue

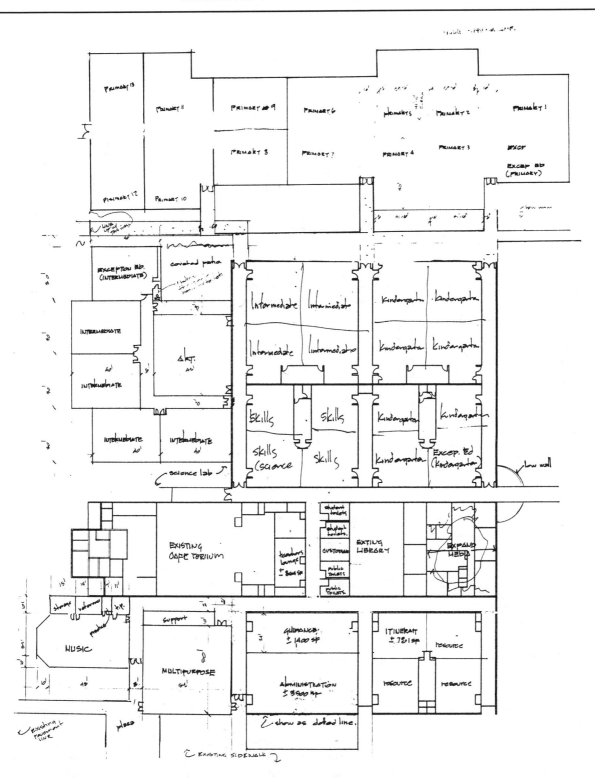

Fig. 13. Existing school plant and library media center. Markham Elementary School, Pompano Beach, Fla.

focused on a series of drawings, the first of which represented the architect's initial conceptualization (see fig. 16).

The drawings enabled continuation of discussions begun during the school visits when requests were made of the architect to include features that would

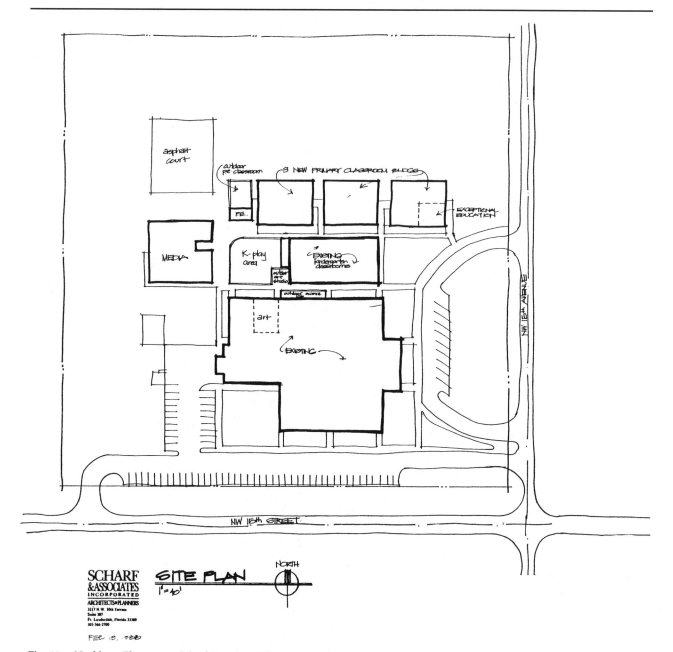

Fig. 14. Markham Elementary School Drawing, February 19, 1988

provide relief from square and rectangular shapes, and that would market the program to the rest of the school and to the community. A curved wall was the response. Now the school planning team wanted to know if brick glass or glass block could be used in the curved wall for security, for diffused light, and for dramatic impact. This request was considered and ultimately included.

The drawing also generated requests for removal of walls and the opening of spaces to provide better circulation and traffic patterns. The opening of spaces would help to preserve the integrity of the library media center when enrollment increased and classroom space was being sought. (A closed-walled room is a readily available "classroom.") Additional drawings and more tissue-paper overlays were used to depict the emerging layout. The sketches on tissue paper represented adjacencies, approximate densities of areas, and possible configurations for the new library media center (see fig. 17).

There still was not a drawing representative of the pattern the school planning team desired. Several

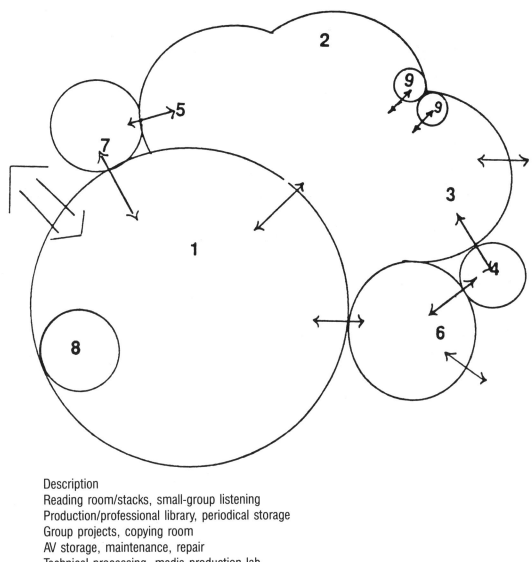

Area	Description
1	Reading room/stacks, small-group listening
2	Production/professional library, periodical storage
3	Group projects, copying room
4	AV storage, maintenance, repair
5	Technical processing, media production lab
6	Closed-circuit TV, closed-circuit storage
7	Library office
8	Conference room
9	Staff toilet

Fig. 15. Space chart for Markham Elementary School

types of built-in furniture had been described in the educational specifications. The school team wanted built-in counters and desks rather than walls to delineate areas in the library media center. Finally, an acceptable tissue overlay emerged and became a drawing (see fig. 18).

At this point, discussion centered on the southern exposure of windows and glass on the perimeter wall of the reading room/stack area. The school planning team was concerned about the effects of

the tropical sun and heat build-up, and light that can be too bright and create glare. Since this wall would have windows above the shelving, it was mutually agreeable to flip the entire plan, placing the reading room/stack area to the north of the allocated space. An acceptable floor plan emerged (see fig. 19).

The plan key in the lower right corner of figure 19 shows space covered in detail on the drawing. It is possible to see the walkways from the rest of the school on this drawing. Because cold weather is not

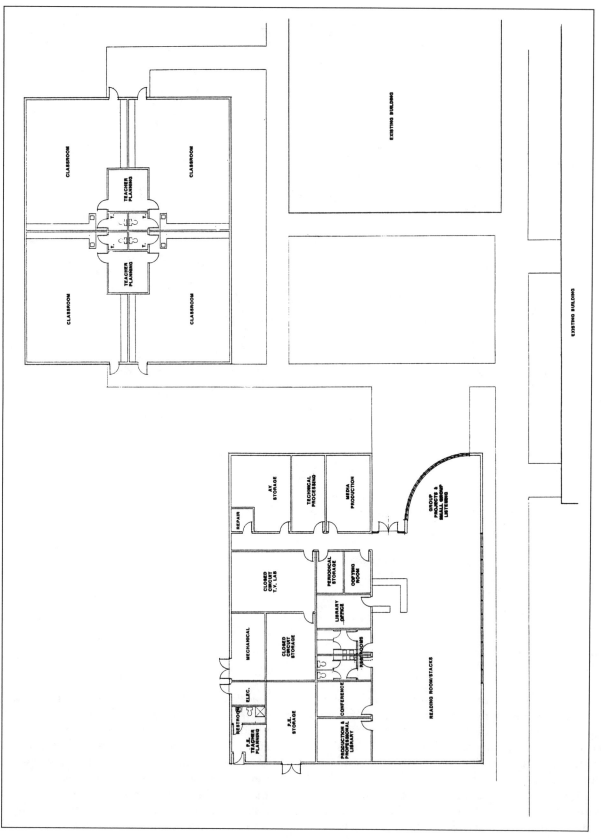

Fig. 16. Markham Elementary School drawing

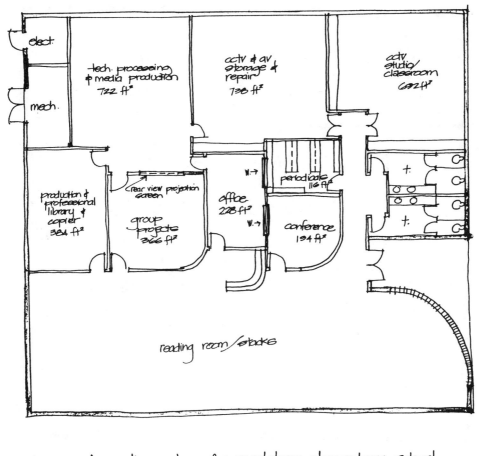

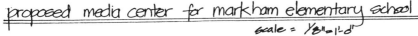

Fig. 17. **Proposed media center for Markham Elementary School**

Layouts

Following acceptance of the drawings, it was time to begin layouts in preparation for construction documents. Layout kits, plastic templates, layout services from library furniture manufacturers, and computer-assisted design programs for the microcomputer are all available to assist planners with this step. The shelving and furniture layout for Markham Elementary School was prepared by the school planning team using templates. The school team had information on current and future collection sizes, curriculum and program emphases, and the district's and school's philosophy. The school team's involvement was also necessary since the district bids its library

a factor, this walkway is canopy-covered for rain and sun protection, and is not enclosed as a hallway or corridor might be.

media furniture and shelving and does not include it in the architect's or general contractor's contract.

Layouts were prepared using nonpermanent spray adhesive and templates. These templates (see Appendix F) were placed on the ¼-inch-scale floor plan. The use of nonpermanent adhesive allows movement of the template pieces to accommodate changes that occur as the layout develops. When a final layout was completed by the school team, it was covered with a sheet of Mylar to prevent sticking when the plans were folded or rolled. This layout, dubbed a "paste-up," was then presented to the architect to be drawn for blueprints.

Upon receiving the paste-up, or layout, from the school team, the architect completed the layout drawings (see fig. 20). These blueprints provided final opportunity to determine if all criteria of the educational specifications had been met.

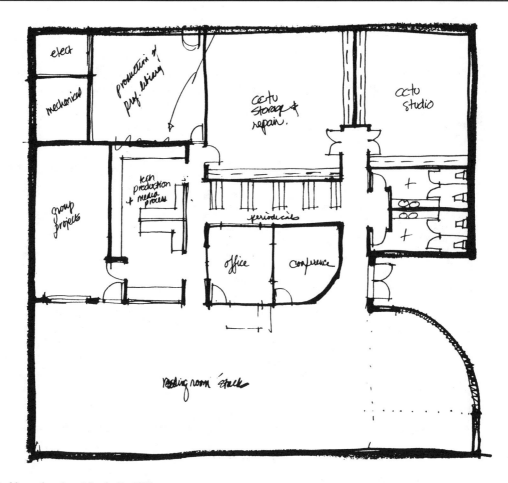

Fig. 18. Markham drawing, March 18, 1988

The school team used this layout to indicate where finished electrical outlets would be needed in the floor's grid system and to locate television antenna outlets for the closed-circuit television system and the instructional television station. There was some time between this phase and completion of the construction documents.

Construction Documents

Detailed construction drawings are intended for the contractor and guide the actual construction. The school planning team must also examine these drawings in order to ensure that function will follow form. At this point, the school team reviewed elevations, electrical drawings, and the elevations of built-in cabinets (see fig. 21).

Determining whether the drawings met the criteria of the educational specifications was the task of the school planning team. This was the final opportunity for changes from the school team since the construction would now be bid and work would begin. The school planning team had completed a good portion of its task.

Construction began with the award of a contract to a general contractor. The district, among the ten largest in the nation, has a large division devoted solely to facilities. The facilities department has its own organizational chart with an associate superintendent at the helm; a director of facilities; designers, including architects, engineers, and draftspersons; document specialists; construction supervisors; and project managers. The project manager for Markham Elementary School was the contact for the professional educators on the school planning team. The project manager was the "owner's representative" for the school board and remained on the scene throughout the construction. In this situation, school staff were not allowed on construction sites except with permission and only for extenuating circumstances.

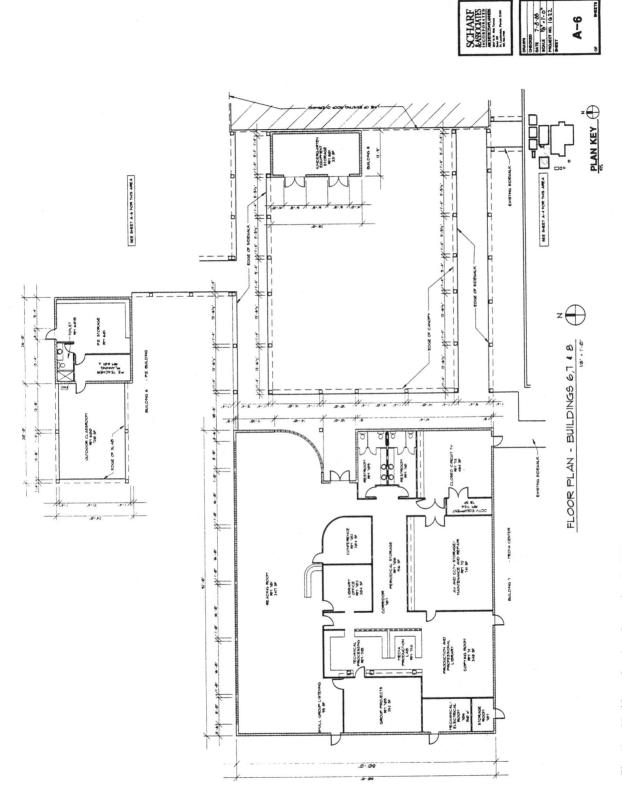

Fig. 19. Markham drawing, September 8, 1988

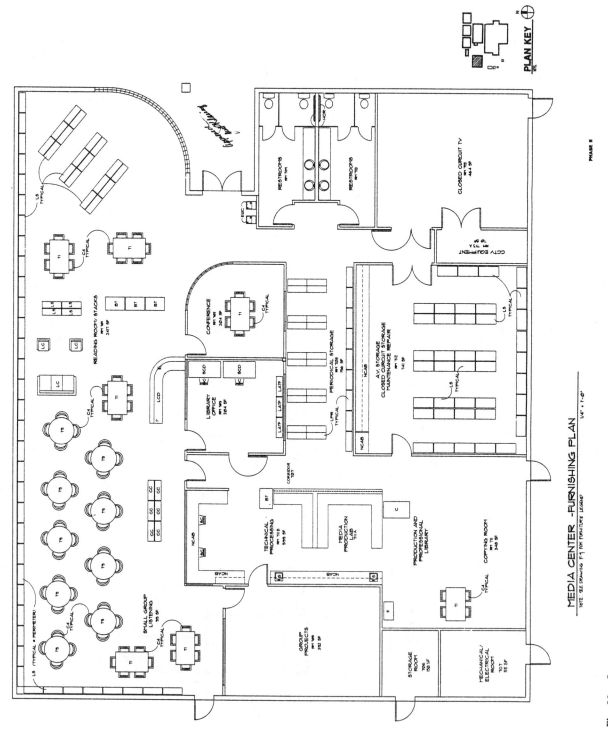

Fig. 20. Layout

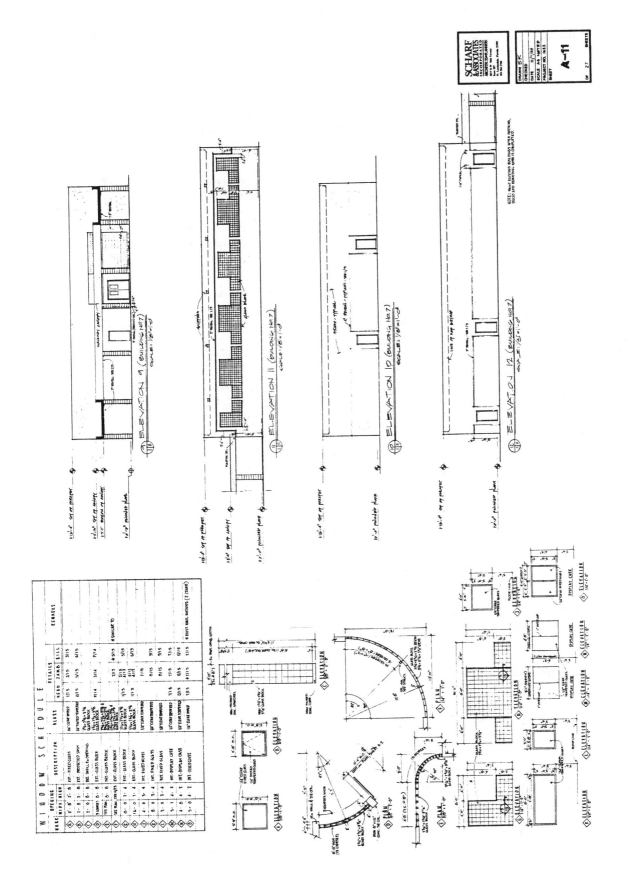

Fig. 21. Detailed construction drawings—window schedule

The project manager continually checked the progress against the drawings. It is easy to understand the importance of the written document—the educational specifications. The document had to be comprehensive and present a strong statement because the drawings and, subsequently, the construction were driven by the educational specifications.

Furniture and Shelving Bid

When construction was eight months from completion, the furniture and shelving bids were prepared by the supervisor responsible for school library media programs. The competitive bid process is time consuming but very cost-effective. In such a large school district, competitive bidding eliminates commission add-ons to cost for both architect and general contractors and makes library furniture rather than classroom furniture in the library media center a possibility. Typically, a minimum of five schools' furniture and shelving are bundled and bid together to take advantage of reduction in costs due to large volume. Since there were no other projects scheduled for completion close to the time of Markham Elementary School, the invitations to bid were sent for this school alone. A time frame of eight months provided time for the bid process, accommodated the school board's schedule of meetings, allowed award of the bid, and provided appropriate time for manufacture, delivery, and installation.

The competitive bid for Markham Elementary School (see Appendix D) included technical writing for equipment for which no models existed. The computer circulation desk module and special carrels were the result of technical descriptive writing. The possibility of many units to be purchased by the school district forced the major manufacturers to respond to the need for such a module for the circulation desk in particular (see fig. 22).

Installation and Evaluation

Once the bid was awarded, it was the responsibility of the supervisor for library media programs to monitor the progress of the furniture and shelving manufacturer and set a schedule for delivery and installation. When the shipment arrived, the delivery was checked against the items specified on the bid, and the furniture was checked for any damage. The shelving was installed as shown on the layout, except for minor adjustments that needed to be made when actual construction dimensions did not match those of the drawings. Such adjustments are made in the field at the time of installation and are typical. Construction, when completed, is frequently not exact. Two 3-foot sections of shelving had to be relocated to available wall space in the production/professional library area.

Final inspection of the shelving included checking the weld joints, identifying any uprights or shelves requiring touch-up paint, and identifying any joints or seams on the shelving base plates and laminate tops that were not flush. The installation went well and was completed in two days. Markham Elementary School's installation was one of high quality and the payment and performance bond was promptly released by the school district.

The facility was now complete, and the move into the library media center was scheduled. The school library media specialist effectively involved the schoolchildren and the community in the excitement of the move. A human chain was formed from the temporary library media center (a former kindergarten classroom), out into the corridors, around corners, past the new kindergarten play area, and into the new center. Shelves were labeled and books were removed from the temporary shelving in classification order, and handed book by book down the chain of celebrants. It was a moment of school and community pride and did much to create excitement for the new facility and the library media program.

The move was completed, and several months of operation provided the appropriate time for preparation of a final list of items to be corrected and additional outlets to be installed, identification of features that were inoperable or did not operate properly, and suggestions for changes in the educational specifications in preparation for the next school. In total, this particular school construction project presented positive experiences and produced a facility with flexibility throughout.

The Markham Elementary School renovation and new construction helped prepare the district for an unprecedented amount of construction and also established a case for improved facilities in all school communities. There is community pride in the Markham Elementary School; children respect and show great care for the facility. There is excitement in the air as children arrive at the library media center, and it is contagious. Construction of a facility such as the Markham Elementary School library media center makes an architectural and program impact upon the school and the community it serves. It speaks to people who have few structures

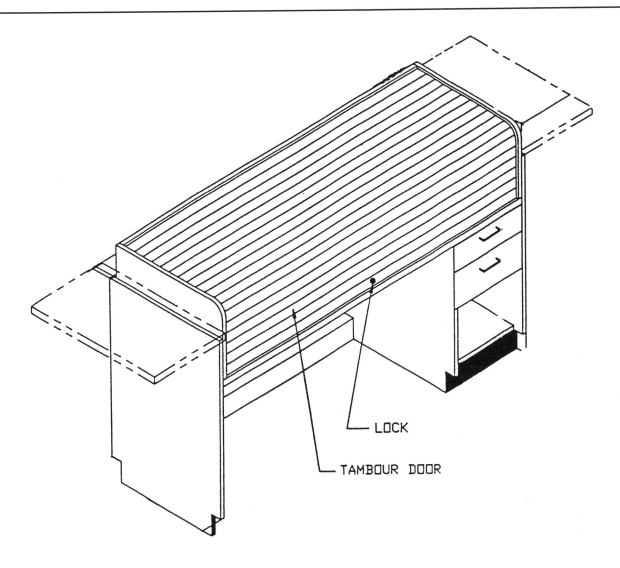

Fig. 22. Circulation desk module—computer unit

of real beauty in their environs; it speaks to school-children and staff as the facility allows creative program activities and provides an attractive environment in which to find information. The school population senses attention will not end with the construction. District level staff, the school board, and the community are looking beyond the facility to the school's becoming a model for program and improved academic performance. Markham Elementary School has the potential to be a pacesetter within the school district. The school responds to the "value conclusions" Robert Propst uses to identify those schools that meet the challenges of the dynamics of education:

Will the schoolhouse be a humane place?
Will it nurture the educative process?
Can it accommodate the future?[1]

Reference

1. Robert Propst, *High School: The Process and the Place* (New York: Educational Facilities Laboratories, 1972), 117. This report was edited by Ruth Weinstock.

SIX

Complexities and Conclusions

Building new facilities is inherently positive, and the beneficial effects on students, staff, and community are undeniable. Whether the school library media center serves a lower socioeconomic community or one of great wealth doesn't matter; as a result of being involved in the construction of more than seventy school library media centers, I have been able to observe the social and psychological effects of new construction. There is an increase in the self-esteem of the students and staff when facilities are renovated or replaced. The surrounding political-geographic community has new pride, and trust in school officials is renewed or strengthened. The quality of the educational program itself is examined when construction is contemplated.

When new schools are built in a community that has older facilities reflecting the educational philosophy of previous decades, issues of parity surface. Both students and staff in the older facility are affected negatively if they perceive they are working with less. Excellent school library media programs can flourish in older facilities, but if the staff are negatively affected by their surroundings, their confidence begins to decline and initiative diminishes. It is important, therefore, not only to meet the need for additional school facilities when growth occurs but also to consider the condition and effectiveness of

the existing buildings serving populations in the same community or district.

The Broward County experience has spawned every possible complexity. For the past several years, rapid, uncontrolled, and unexpected growth has generated the need for classrooms and support facilities for more than 6,000 additional students annually. To meet this need, the construction program has included well-planned facilities, fast-track projects, and renovations. Even a restaurant has been converted to serve as an elementary school.

Typically, no library media specialist is hired in advance of the opening of a new Broward County school, creating unique problems in the planning process. The educational specifications documents have become critical. Committees of school library media specialists worked with the district administrative staff to develop detailed educational specifications. These are revised annually and are evaluated as the results of the specifications—the new or renovated school library media centers—are examined.

The dynamics of this planning experience in Broward County schools reveal a microcosm of the human factors that can arise. There are architects who are receptive and encourage dialogue, architects who take ownership of a design before dialogue has taken place and resist suggestions for change, and architects who would prefer that school library media specialists prepare the drawings. There are school administrators and principals with different leadership styles and experiences who broaden or limit the possibilities for creative design. There are school library media specialists who bring a wide variety of experiences to the planning process, and those who, for many reasons, have not kept pace with the changes in delivery systems and resources. Developing a plan that enables the library media program to meet the guidelines of *Information Power* will take every communication and research skill to which the library media professional has been exposed. The educational specifications developed by the school planning team will meet the unique needs of the individual school program, staff, and community as well as geographic constraints. The school planning team will provide the initial stimulus for the design team. The description of program requirements in the educational specifications will spawn the facility's design when these two teams work in concert—the school planning team articulating current and future program needs and the architectural design team creatively responding to the educational specifications. Dialogue with those who will work in the school library media center for many years after the architectural firm has left the scene is essential to the process. The effects of this partnership will last for the life of the building.

The school library media center program requires that flexibility be inherent in the design. The facility must accommodate continuous change as the program and staff respond to an evolving curriculum, the impact of technologies yet unknown, and the diverse needs of students, teachers, and the community. School library media professionals must articulate the evolutionary patterns of school library media programs, be futurists in the school community, and guide the planning process for new and renovated facilities that will meet the needs of several generations to come.

GLOSSARY FOR
SCHOOL LIBRARY MEDIA SPECIALISTS

Additive/Alternate Work requiring detailed cost analysis at time of construction bid but which may or may not be part of the project depending on availability of funds.

Adjacency diagram Another term for "bubble diagram."

Bubble diagram A diagram that uses different geometric forms to depict required spaces and their functional or physical relationships. Developed by the school planning team.

CAD Computer-aided design approach to planning. Computer program used by architectural firm.

Change order An alteration to a construction contract after the contract has been approved and amended, and the project is under construction.

Completion, final The date when the architect declares that all work has been completed and all deficiencies corrected, and that everything is acceptable in accordance with the contract documents.

Completion, substantial The date that the work or designated portion of the work is certified by the architect as being sufficiently complete so the school district may occupy the facility.

Construction The creation of something new, rather than repair or improvement of something existing.

Construction documents phase Consists primarily of the final drawings, specifications, and bidding documents.

Construction program document Consists of narrative description of entire construction project and is basis for requests for proposals or invitations to bid by architectural firms and general contractors.

Design development phase Preparation of more detailed preliminary drawings than schematic design phase. Includes supporting data.

Floor plan Drawings accurately drafted and showing placement of walls, doors, and windows. Includes square footage in a small, rectangular box for each main area on the drawing. May include equipment and furnishing layouts.

Head-end equipment Distribution equipment for closed-circuit television. Includes modulators, amplifiers, switching equipment.

Key plan A small, descriptive plan of entire site that highlights location of the individual building or room shown on drawing.

Lens, parabolic, paracube Special lens covering light fixtures to reduce glare on work surfaces.

Project manager A representative of the school governing agency, sometimes known as "project engineer" or "clerk of the works." Retained on the job on a full-time basis, mainly for inspection purposes that are beyond the scope of normal architectural services.

Renovation Repair or improvement of something already existing.

Scale Dimension used to express relative proportion of linear feet.

Schematic design phase Study by the architect of project requirements, followed by the preparation of schematic design drawings and supporting data. Drawings are not to scale.

Site plan Shows entire site at suitable scale with boundary lines and orientation. Includes topographic information, building layout, drives, parking areas, walks, play areas.

GLOSSARY FOR ARCHITECTS

Carrel, wet   Individual workstation area providing a work space approximately 3' × 3' with mechanical core providing electricity and electronics networking.

CD-ROM   Compact disc computer technology used to store large volumes of information, both audio and visual.

Communications network   The system by which a group of nodes interconnect for the transmission of data.

Computer, host   Computer to which terminals are connected through a communications network.

Database   A collection of data in machine-readable form.

Distance learning   Educational programs transmitted by computer, telephone, or television satellite systems permitting learner access to programs at different geographic locations.

Head-end equipment   Distribution equipment for closed-circuit television. Includes modulators, amplifiers, switching equipment.

Library media specialist   A person with certification and broad professional preparation, both in education and library media, with competencies to carry out a media program. The library media specialist is the media professional in the school program.

Modem   A peripheral device used to connect computers and terminals. Transmission by telephone connections enables transfer of information from one computer to another.

Network   Provides the communication links between a series of computers and user terminals.

Online   Retrieval of information by direct, interactive communication between the user at a terminal and the computer, programmed to provide access to databases.

OPAC   An acronym for "public access catalog"; interchangeably used for an online or microcomputer catalog.

Public access catalog   A computer index of school library media center materials by author, subject, and title. Permits rapid searching and location of bibliographic entries.

School library media center   An area or system of areas in the school where a full range of information resources, materials, equipment, and services are accessible to students, school staff, and the educational community.

School library media program   The instructional objectives, activities, facilities, resources, equipment, and staff that are used to assist students and staff.

Telecommunications   The exchange of information by electrical transmission.

SELECTED READINGS

Planning and Designing School Library Media Center Facilities

American Association of School Librarians and Association for Educational Communications and Technology. *Information Power.* Chicago: American Library Association; and Washington, D.C.: Association for Educational Communications and Technology, 1988.

Anderson, Pauline. *Planning School Library Media Facilities.* Hamden, Conn.: Library Professional Publications, 1990.

Boss, Richard W. *Information Technologies and Space Planning for Libraries and Information Centers.* Boston: G. K. Hall, 1987.

Chase, Bill. "Drawing Strength: Skillful Design . . . and a Little Trickery." *School Library Journal* 36 (February 1990): 21-25.

Cohen, Aaron, and Elaine Cohen. *Designing and Space Planning for Libraries: A Behavioral Guide.* New York: Bowker, 1979.

Dahlgren, Anders C., ed. "Library Buildings." *Library Trends* 36, no. 2 (Fall 1987): 261-491.

Dahlgren, Anders C., and Erla Beck, comps. *Planning Library Buildings: A Select Bibliography.* Chicago: Library Administration and Management Association/American Library Association, 1990.

Educational Facilities Laboratory. *The Secondary School: Reduction, Renewal, and Real Estate: A Report from Educational Facilities Laboratories.* New York: Educational Facilities Laboratories, 1976.

Ellsworth, Ralph, and Hobart Wagener. *The School Library: Facilities for Independent Study in the Secondary School.* New York: Educational Facilities Laboratories, 1963.

Fraley, Ruth A. *Library Space Planning.* New York: Neal-Schuman, 1985.

Hannigan, Jane A. "Charette: Media Facilities Design." *School Media Quarterly* 2, no. 3 (Spring 1974): 185-294.

Hannigan, Jane Anne, and Glenn Estes, comps. and eds. *Media Center Facilities Design.* Chicago: American Library Association, 1978.

Katz, William A., and Roderick G. Swartz, eds. *Problems in Planning Library Facilities.* Chicago: American Library Association, 1964.

Kelsey, F. Lamar. "School Design That Lifts Minds and Spirit." *The School Administrator* 46, no. 6 (June 1989): 18-20.

Lamkin, Bernice. "A Media Center for the 21st Century." *School Library Journal* 33, no. 3 (November 1986): 25-29.

Lucker, Jay K. "Adapting Libraries to Current and Future Needs." *Library Hi Tech* 5, no. 4 (Winter 1987): 87.

Lushington, Nolan, and Willis N. Mills, Jr. *Libraries Designed for Users: A Planning Handbook.* Hamden, Conn.: Library Professional Publications, 1980.

Propst, Robert. *High School: The Process and the Place.* New York: Educational Facilities Laboratories, 1972.

Rohlf, Robert. "Library Design: What Not to Do." *American Libraries* 17, no. 2 (February 1986): 100-104.

Roth, Harold L., ed. *Planning Library Buildings for Service.* Chicago: American Library Association, 1984.

Schulzetenberg, Anthony C. "Building and Remodeling School Media Facilities to Accommodate the New Technologies." *School Library Media Annual 1984, Volume Two*, ed. Shirley L. Aaron and Pat R. Scales. Littleton, Colo.: Libraries Unlimited, 1984, 469-79.

Smith, Lester K., ed. *Planning Library Buildings: From Decision to Design.* Chicago: American Library Association, 1986.

Tregloan, Don. "Designing Your Instructional Center." *Media and Methods* 26, no. 2 (November/December 1989): 24-27f.

Weinstock, Ruth. *The Greening of the High School: A Report on a Conference.* New York: Educational Facilities Laboratory, 1973.

Working with the Architect and the Consultant

Buchanan, George. "By Design: It's All in the Details." *School Library Journal* 36 (February 1990): 25-27.

Lewis, Myron E., and Mark L. Nelson. "How to Work With an Architect." *Wilson Library Bulletin* 57, no. 1 (September 1982): 44-46.

Library Administration and Management Association. *Library Buildings Consultant List.* Chicago: American Library Association, 1989.

Rohlf, Robert H. "Best-Laid Plans: A Consultant's Constructive Advice." *School Library Journal* 36 (February 1990): 28-31.

Shaffer, Kenneth R. "Library Consultant: Who? When? Why." *School Media Quarterly* 2, no. 3 (Spring 1974): 213-16.

The Technical Considerations

Architectural Woodwork Institute. *Architectural Woodwork Quality Standards, Guide Specifications and Quality Certification Program.* Arlington, Va.: Architectural Woodwork Institute, 1989.

Architectural Woodwork Institute. *Guide to Wood Species.* Arlington, Va.: Architectural Woodwork Institute, 1977.

Hill, Franklin. *Tomorrow's Learning Environment, Planning Technology: The Basics.* Alexandria, Va.: National School Board Association, 1988.

McQueen, Judy, and Richard W. Boss. "Interfacing Products for Libraries." *Library Technology Reports* 25, no. 4 (July/August 1988): 505-605.

Packard, Robert T., and Stephen A. Kliment, eds. *Architectural Graphic Standards Student Edition.* New York: Wiley, 1988.

Saffady, William. "The Cost of Automated Cataloging Support: An Analysis and Comparison of Selected Products and Services." *Library Trends* 25, no. 4 (July/August 1989): 461-631.

The Environment

Bennett, Jim. "Trends in School Library Media Facilities, Furnishings, and Collections." *Library Trends* 36, no. 2 (Fall 1987): 317-25.

Draper, James, and James Brooks. *Interior Design for Libraries.* Chicago: American Library Association, 1979.

Pollett, Dorothy, and Peter Haskell, eds. *Sign System for Solving the Wayfinding Problems.* New York: Bowker, 1979.

The Furniture

Brown, Carol R. *Selecting Library Furniture: A Guide for Librarians, Designers and Architects.* Phoenix, Ariz.: Oryx Press, 1989.

Dellamore, John J. "Designing the Next Generation of Library Automation Furniture." *Library Administration and Management* 2, no. 1 (January 1988): 42.

Friedman, Rick. "Free-Standing Work Station Systems Are Now in Vogue." *The Office* 105, no. 6 (June 1987): 76.

Kenney, Donald, and Linda Wilson. "Online Catalogs: Some Ergonomic Considerations." *Wilson Library Bulletin* 63, no. 4 (December 1988): 46-48.

Martin, Ron G. "Design Considerations for an OPAC Workstation: An Introduction to Specifications and a Model Configuration." *Library Hi Tech* 7, no. 4 (Consecutive Issue 28, 1989): 19-27.

Michaels, Andrea Arthur. "Standard Lines or Custom-Designed?" *American Libraries* 19, no. 4 (April 1988): 267-69.

Novak, Gloria. "Working Within the Systems; Office-Landscape Furniture Systems Create Order Out of Computer Chaos." *American Libraries* 19, no. 4 (April 1988): 270-71.

Poole, Frazer G., and Alphonse F. Trezza, eds. *The Procurement of Library Furnishings: Specifications, Bid Documents and Evaluation.* Chicago: American Library Association, 1969.

Vasi, John. "Staff Furnishings for Libraries." *Library Trends* 87, no. 2 (Fall 1987): 389-99.

Weese, Ben. "Furnishings Can Surprise and Delight." *American Libraries* 19, no. 4 (April 1988): 272, 297-98.

Werdlin, Lynette. "Moving a Collection." *The Book Report* 6, no. 5 (March/April 1988): 28.

APPENDIX A

Construction of a Bubble Diagram

The bubble diagram will show spatial relationships and proportionate sizes of individual areas to the whole. Whether ovals, circles, or some other geometric forms are used, the message relayed by the bubble diagram will be understood by the architectural team. The geometric form will define space and function:

- Closed figures indicate separate and distinct functions requiring a closed area or room.
- Figures that do not touch each other signal the need for corridors between.

- Figures that touch one another indicate the need for immediate adjacency.
- Figures that overlap show areas that must be accessible, or flow from one area into the other.
- Figures that flow into one another depict spaces that are not distinctly separated by walls, but allow continuous flow in large, open, areas.
- Connecting arrows indicate the need for passage between areas.

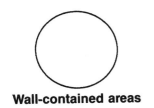

Wall-contained areas

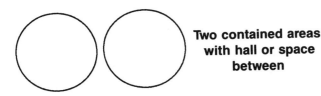

Two contained areas with hall or space between

Two contained areas sharing the same wall

71

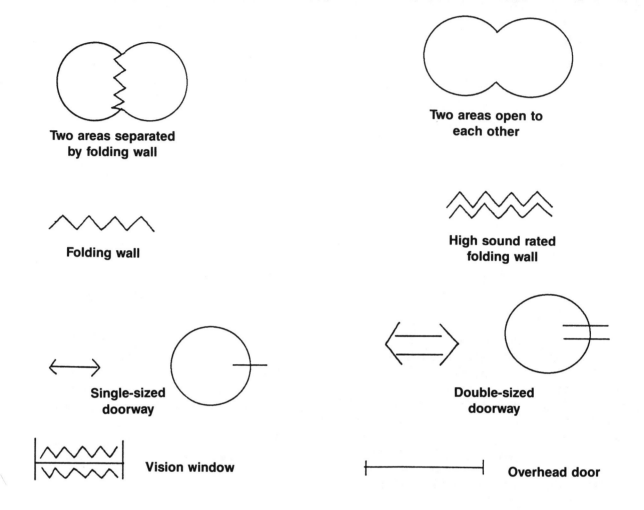

Two areas separated
by folding wall

Two areas open to
each other

Folding wall

High sound rated
folding wall

Single-sized
doorway

Double-sized
doorway

Vision window

Overhead door

APPENDIX B

Architectural Symbols for the Library Media Specialist

Symbols that commonly appear in construction drawings should be readily recognized by the school library media specialist in preparation for dialogue with the architectural planning team.

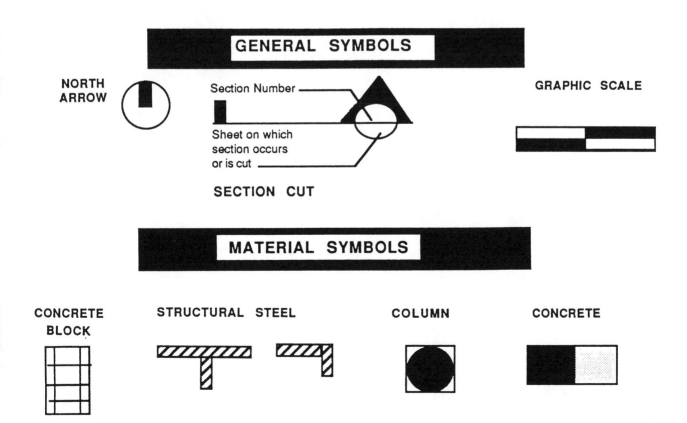

PLAN SYMBOLS

GLASS BLOCK

CONCRETE BLOCK W/COLUMN

WINDOW & MARK

EXISTING TO BE REMOVED

EXISTING CONSTRUCTION TO REMAIN

DOOR & MARK

120 volt 20A
Duplex Receptacle
Floor

120 volt 20A
Duplex Receptacle
Mounted

COMPUTER OUTLET

C

Telephone Outlet

Telephone Outlet
Floor Mounted

**FIRE ALARM
PULL STATION**

P

**FIRE ALARM
HORN & STROBE**

H

Television Junction Box
Mounted as Required

TV

APPENDIX C

Basic Equipment Checklist

Items from the following list of equipment might be included in the library media center's inventory. Because school staff will continue to use familiar resources and equipment and film libraries will continue to circulate motion pictures even when they may have added video formats and language magnetic-card readers will continue to resurface in schools serving multilingual populations, the list includes traditional equipment as well as the newest technology. The checklist is available for school planning teams that must place orders for equipment under capital funding during a construction program, and will help eliminate oversights in the purchasing process.

Quantity	Item Description
_____ per school	Amplifier (sound system), portable
_____ per media center	Book detection system (electronic security system)
_____ per media center	Calculator, electric print
_____ per media center	Camcorder
_____ per media center	Camera, 35mm w/flash
_____ per media center	Camera (35mm) tripod
_____ per _____ teaching stations _____ per media center	Cart, Projection, 26"
_____ per _____ teaching stations _____ per media center	Cart, Projection, 34"

Quantity	Item Description
_____ per_____ teaching stations _____ per media center	Cart for television receiver
_____ per media center	Chair, Secretary
_____ per media center	Library computer/hard disc system—automated circulation and inventory
_____ per media center	Computer, monitor, printer (patron workstation)
_____ per media center	Computer, with graphics capability, Printer (patron workstation)
_____ per media center	Computer workstation/CD-ROM Bibliographic databases
_____ per media center	Computer workstation/CD-ROM Public access computer catalog

Quantity	Item Description	Quantity	Item Description
_____ per media center	Computer workstation/CD-ROM Reference databases	_____ per media center	Lettering device (mechanical)
_____ per media center	Computer workstation Interactive video	_____ per media center	Lighting kit (portable 110V)
_____ per media center	Computer table	_____ per media center	Listening jack strip
_____ per media center	Conference table	_____ per media center	Magnetic card reader
_____ per remedial lab _____ per media center	Controlled reader	_____ per media center	Microform cabinet
_____ per media center	Copy machine—book copier and transparency maker	_____ per media center	Microform reader/printer (roll & fiche)
_____ per media center	Copy machine (xerographic process)	_____ per media center	Photo processor
		_____ per media center	Photo timer, minute
_____ per media center	Copystand, camera	_____ per media center	Photographic paper safe
_____ per media center	Cutter, rotary paper, 25½"	_____ per media center	Plastic bottles, one gallon, brown
_____ per media center	Developing tank and film washers, automatic	_____ per media center	Plastic bottles, one quart, brown
_____ per media center	Drymount press	_____ per media center	Plastic photo trays, 11" × 14"
_____ per media center	Easel, folding display	_____ per media center	Pointer
_____ per media center	Electronic security system (building security)	_____ per media center	Print dryer
		_____ per media center	Programmer, multi-image
_____ per media center	Fax machine	_____ per media center	Projector, analysis, 16mm
_____ per media center	File, lateral 4-drawer (n/lock)	_____ per_____ teaching stations _____ per media center	Projector, 16mm
_____ per media center	File, lateral 4-drawer (w/lock)		
_____ per_____ teaching stations _____ per media center	Filmstrip/cassette combination (front and rear projection)	_____ per_____ teaching stations _____ per media center	Projector, filmstrip
_____ per media center	Headsets	_____ per_____ teaching stations _____ per media center	Projector, filmstrip/cassette combination
_____ per media center	Jack strips	_____ per media center	Projector, opaque
_____ per media center	Laminating machine, 25"	_____ per_____ teaching stations _____ per media center	Projector, overhead
_____ per media center	Language lab		
_____ per media center	LCD computer projector panel		

Quantity	Item Description	Quantity	Item Description
_____ per_____ teaching stations _____ per media center	Projector, slide carousel	_____ per media center	Tape recorder, cassette, heavy duty w/synchronizer
_____ per_____ teaching stations _____ per media center	Projector, slide/cassette combination	_____ per_____ teaching stations _____ per media center	Tape recorder, playback only
_____ per media center	Rack, multi-image	_____ per media center	Tape recorder, reel to reel
_____ per_____ teaching stations _____ per media center	Record player, classroom	_____ per media center	Telefacsimile equipment
		_____ per media center	Telephone modem
_____ per media center	Record player, stereo	_____ per media center	Television/audio distribution equipment
_____ per media center	Record player, variable speed	_____ per media center	Television camera mounting system
_____ per media center	Safe lights		
_____ per media center	Scanner	_____ per_____ teaching stations _____ per media center	Television receiver, color, 25"
_____ per media center	Screen, rearview		
_____ per media center	Screen, tripod, 60" × 60"	_____ per media center	Television studio camera ensemble
_____ per_____ teaching stations _____ per media center	Screen, wall, 60" × 60"	_____ per media center	Transparency maker
		_____ per media center	Typewriter, electric, with memory
_____ per school	Screen, auditorium, 12' × 12'	_____ per media center	Vacuum cleaner (hand, rechargeable)
_____ per media center	Security anchor pad		
_____ per media center	Sound system, portable w/lavalier mike	_____ per media center	Video color printer
_____ per media center	Stools (on casters)	_____ per media center	Video display projector, large screen
_____ per media center	Stools (n/back)	_____ per media center	Video system, interactive
_____ per media center	Surge suppressor	_____ per media center	Video tape editor
_____ per media center	Tachistoscope	_____ per media center	Video tape eraser
_____ per_____ teaching stations _____ per media center	Tape recorder/playback, classroom	_____ per media center	Video tape player
		_____ per media center	Video tape recorder
_____ per_____ teaching stations _____ per media center	Tape recorder, cassette, heavy duty	_____ per media center	Videodisc player
		_____ per media center	Wireless microphone

APPENDIX D

Sample Furniture and Shelving Bid
and
Bid Analysis Matrix

| The School Board of Broward County, Florida
PURCHASING DEPARTMENT
1320 Southwest Fourth Street
Fort Lauderdale, Florida 33312-7535 | **INVITATION TO BID**
Bidder Acknowledgement |

INVITATION TO BID
Bidder Acknowledgement

| Telephone Number — Purchasing
(305) 765-6120 | **Bid Number:** 90-137S | **Date Mailed:** 6/28/89 |

Bids will be opened in the Purchasing Department at 2:00 P.M. on

JULY 12, 1989

and may not be withdrawn within sixty (60) days after such date and time.

BID TITLE: FURNISH & INSTALL NEW LIBRARY SHELVING AND FURNITURE – MARKHAM ELEMENTARY SCHOOL

Vendor Name:

Terms: Bidder see P 3 - General Conditions

Vendor Mailing Address:

In order for Bids to be considered for award, Bidder **MUST** return with Bid submitted the executed Invitation to Bid form plus **all required** Bid Summary Sheet pages, all other required pages, and other required submittals as described herein.

City - State - Zip Code:

VENDOR TAXPAYER IDENTIFICATION NUMBER

| Telephone Number:
Area Code: | Toll-Free Number:
1-800- | Facsimile Number:
Area Code: |

I certify that this bid is made without prior understanding, agreement or connection with any corporation, firm or person submitting a bid for the same materials, supplies, or equipment and is in all respects fair and without collusion or fraud. I certify acceptance of all Conditons, Specifications, and other information attached hereto. I certify that I am authorized to sign this bid for the bidder.

I agree that this bid cannot be withdrawn within sixty (60) days from date due.

Signature of Authorized Representative (Manual)

Name of Authorized Representative (Typed or Printed)　　　Title

GENERAL CONDITIONS
Bidder: To insure acceptance of the bid follow these instructions —

1. **SEALED BID REQUIREMENTS:** The "INVITATION TO BID" sheet must be completed, signed, and returned with the bid. The "SWORN STATEMENT UNDER SECTION 287.133(3)(a), FLORIDA STATUTES, ON PUBLIC ENTITY CRIMES" must be completed, signed, NOTARIZED, and returned as described herein. The Bid Summary Sheet pages on which the bidder actually submits a bid and any pages upon which information is required to be inserted must be completed and submitted with the bid. **Bids received that fail to comply with these submittal requirements shall not be considered for award.**

   a) **BIDDER'S RESPONSIBILITY:** It is the responsibility of the bidder to be certain that all numbered pages of the Bid and all attachments thereto are received; and all Addendum released are received prior to submitting a bid. All bids are subject to the conditions specified herein, on the attached Bid documents, and on any Addendum issued thereto.

   b) **BID SUBMITTED:** Completed bid must be submitted sealed in an envelope. Bids must be time stamped in the Purchasing Department **prior to 2:00 p.m. on date due.** No bid will be considered if not time stamped in the Purchasing Department prior to 2:00 pm on date due. Bids will be opened at 2:00 pm on date due. Bids submitted by telegraphic or facsimile transmission, including any literature or other attachments associated therewith, will not be accepted.

   c) **EXECUTION OF BID:** Bid must contain a manual signature of an authorized representative in the space provided above. Failure to properly sign bid shall invalidate same, and it shall **not** be considered for award. All bids must be completed in ink or typewritten. No erasures are permitted. If a correction is necessary, draw a single line through the entered figure and enter the corrected figure above it. Corrections must be initialed by the person signing the bid. Any illegible entries, pencil bids or corrections not initialed will not be tabulated. The original bid conditions and specifications **cannot** be changed or altered in any way. Altered bids will not be considered.

2. **NO BID:** If not submitting a bid, respond by completing and returning one copy of this form, marking it "No bid," and explain below the reason. Failure to bid without sufficient justification shall be cause for removal of a supplier's name from the bid mailing list. **Note: A bidder, to qualify as a respondent, must submit a "no bid" and same must be received no later than the stated bid opening date and hour.**
   Reason for "no bid": _____

3. **PRICES QUOTED:** Deduct trade discounts and quote firm net prices. Give both unit price and extended total. Prices must be stated in units to quantity specified in the bidding specification. In case of discrepancy in computing the amount of the bid, the **Unit Price** quoted will govern. All prices quoted shall be F.O.B. destination, freight prepaid (Bidder pays and bears freight charges. Bidder owns goods in transit and files any claims), unless otherwise stated in Special Conditions. Discounts for prompt payment: Award, if made,

will be in accordance with terms and conditions stated herein. Each item must be bid separately and no attempt is to be made to tie any item or items in with any other item or items. **Cash or quantity discounts offered will not be a consideration in determination of award of bid(s).** If a bidder offers a discount or offers terms less than Net 30, it is understood that a minimum of 30 days will be required for payment, and if a payment discount is offered, the discount time will be computed from the date of satisfactory delivery at place of acceptance and receipt of correct invoice at the office specified.

   a) **TAXES:** The School Board of Broward County, Florida does not pay Federal Excise and State taxes on direct purchases of tangible personal property. The applicable tax exemption number is shown on the purchase order. This exemption does **not** apply to purchases of tangible personal property made by contractors who use the tangible personal property in the performance of contracts for the improvement of School Board owned real property as defined in Chapter 192 of the Florida Statutes.

   b) **MISTAKES:** Bidders are expected to examine the specifications, delivery schedules, bid prices and extensions, and all instructions pertaining to supplies and services. Failure to do so will be at bidder's risk.

   c) **CONDITION AND PACKAGING:** It is understood and agreed that any item offered or shipped as a result of this bid shall be new (current production model at the time of this bid.) All containers shall be suitable for storage or shipment, and all prices shall include standard commercial packaging.

   d) **UNDERWRITERS' LABORATORIES:** Unless otherwise stipulated in the bid, all manufactured items and fabricated assemblies shall be U.L. listed where such has been established by U.L. for the item(s) offered and furnished. In lieu of the U.L. listing, bidder may substitute a listing by an independent testing laboratory recognized by OSHA under the Nationally Recognized Testing Laboratories (NRTL) Recognition Program.

   e) **BIDDER'S CONDITIONS:** The Board specifically reserves the right to reject any conditional bid.

4. **NONCONFORMANCE TO CONTRACT CONDITIONS:** Items offered may be tested for compliance with bid conditions and specifications. Items delivered, not conforming to bid conditions or specifications, may be rejected and returned at vendor's expense. Goods or services not delivered as per delivery date in bid and/or purchase order may be purchased on the open market. Any increase in cost may be charged against the bidder. Any violation of these stipulations may also result in:

   1. Vendor's name being removed from the Department of Purchasing vendor mailing list for two (2) years and vendor not being recommended for any award during this period.
   2. All departments being advised not to do business with vendor.

5. **SAMPLES:** Samples of items, when required, must be furnished free of expense within 5 working days of request unless otherwise stated and, if not destroyed, will, upon request, be returned at the bidder's expense. Bidders will be responsible for the removal of all samples furnished within 30 days after bid opening. All samples will be disposed of after 30 days. Each individual sample must be labeled with bidder's name, bid number, and item number. Failure of bidder to either deliver required samples or to clearly identify samples as indicated may be reason for rejection of the bid. Unless otherwise indicated, samples should be delivered to the office of the Purchasing Department of The School Board of Broward County, Florida, 1320 Southwest Fourth Street, Fort Lauderdale, Florida 33312.

6. **DELIVERY:** Unless actual date of delivery is specified (or if specified delivery cannot be met), show number of days required to make delivery after receipt of purchase order in space provided. Delivery time may become a basis for making an award (see Special Conditions). Delivery shall be within the normal working hours of the user, Monday through Friday, excluding holidays.

7. **INTERPRETATIONS:** Any questions concerning conditions and specifications should be submitted in writing and received by the Department of Purchasing no later than three (3) working days prior to the bid opening. If necessary, an Addendum will be issued.

8. **AWARDS:** In the best interest of the School Board, the Board reserves the right to reject any and all bids and to waive any irregularity in bids received; to accept any item or group of items unless qualified by bidder; to acquire additional quantities at prices quoted on this invitation unless additional quantities are not acceptable, in which case the bid sheets must be noted "BID IS FOR SPECIFIED QUANTITY ONLY." All awards made as a result of this bid shall conform to applicable Florida Statutes.

9. **BID OPENING:** Shall be public, on the date and at the time specified on the bid form. All bids received after that time shall not be considered.

10. **ADVERTISING:** In submitting a proposal, bidder agrees not to use the results therefrom as a part of any commercial advertising without prior approval of the School Board.

11. **INSPECTION, ACCEPTANCE & TITLE:** Inspection and acceptance will be at destination unless otherwise provided. Title to/or risk of loss or damage to all items shall be the responsibility of the successful bidder until acceptance by the buyer unless loss or damage result from negligence by the buyer. If the materials or services supplied to the Board are found to be defective or not conform to specifications, the Board reserves the right to cancel the order upon written notice to the seller and return product at bidder's expense.

12. **PAYMENT:** Payment will be made by the buyer after the items awarded to a vendor have been received, inspected, and found to comply with award specifications, free of damage or defect and properly invoiced.

13. **CONFLICT OF INTEREST:** The award hereunder is subject to the provisions of Chapter 112, Florida Statutes. All bidders must disclose with their bid the name of any officer, director, or agent who is also an employee of the School Board of Broward County, Florida. Further, all bidders must disclose the name of any Board employee who owns, directly or indirectly, an interest of five per cent (5%) or more in the bidder's firm or any of its branches.

14. **DISPUTES:** In case of any doubt or difference of opinion as to the items to be furnished hereunder, the decision of the buyer shall be final and binding on both parties.

15. **LEGAL REQUIREMENTS:** Federal, State, county, and local laws, ordinances, rules, and regulations that in any manner affect the items covered herein apply. Lack of knowledge by the bidder will in no way be a cause for relief from responsibility.

16. **PATENTS & ROYALTIES:** The bidder, without exception, shall indemnify and save harmless The School Board of Broward County, Florida and its employees from liability of any nature or kind, including cost and expenses for or on account of any copyrighted, patented, or unpatented invention, process, or article manufactured or used in the performance of the contract, including its use by The School Board of Broward County, Florida. If the bidder uses any design, device, or materials covered by letters, patent, or copyright, it is mutually understood and agreed without exception that the bid prices shall include all royalties or cost arising from the use of such design, device, or materials in any way involved in the work.

17. **OSHA:** The bidder warrants that the product supplied to The School Board of Broward County, Florida shall conform in all respects to the standards set forth in the Occupational Safety and Health Act of 1970, as amended, and the failure to comply with this condition will be considered as a breach of contract.

18. **SPECIAL CONDITIONS:** The Superintendent has the authority to issue Special Conditions and Specifications as required for individual bids. Any and all Special Conditions that may vary from these General Conditions shall have precedence.

19. **ANTI-DISCRIMINATION:** The bidder certifies that he or she is in compliance with the non-discrimination clause contained in Section 202, Executive Order 11246, as amended by Executive Order 11375, relative to equal employment opportunity for all persons without regard to race, color, religion, sex or national origin.

20. **QUALITY:** All materials used for the manufacture or construction of any supplies, materials or equipment covered by this bid shall be new. The items bid must be new, the latest model, of the best quality, and highest grade workmanship.

21. **LIABILITY, INSURANCE, LICENSES AND PERMITS:** Where bidders are required to enter or go onto School Board property to deliver materials or perform work or services as a result of a bid award, the bidder agrees to the Hold Harmless Agreement stated herein and will assume the full duty obligation and expense of obtaining all necessary licenses, permits and insurance. The bidder shall be liable for any damages or loss to the Board occasioned by negligence of the bidder (or agent) or any person the bidder has designated in the completion of the contract as a result of their bid.

22. **BID BONDS, PERFORMANCE BONDS, CERTIFICATES OF INSURANCE:** Bid bonds, when required, shall be submitted with the bid in the amount specified in Special Conditions. Bid bonds will be returned to unsuccessful bidders. After acceptance of bid, the Board will notify the successful bidder to submit a performance bond and certificate of insurance in the amount specified in Special Conditions. Upon receipt of the performance bond, the bid bond will be returned to the successful bidder.

23. **"DEFAULT -** in the event of default on a contract, the successful bidder shall pay to the Board, as liquidated damages an amount equal to 25% of the unit price bid, times the quantity (or) $50.00, whichever amount is larger. In the event of default on a contract, the successful bidder shall pay all attorney's fees and court costs incurred in collecting any liquidated damages."

24. **CANCELLATION:** In the event any of the provisions of this bid are violated by the contractor, the Superintendent shall give written notice to the contractor stating the deficiencies and unless deficiencies are corrected within five (5) days, recommendation will be made to the School Board for immediate cancellation. The School Board of Broward County, Florida reserves the right to terminate any contract resulting from this invitation at any time and for any reason, upon giving thirty (30) days prior written notice to the other party.

25. **BILLING INSTRUCTIONS:** Invoices, unless otherwise indicated, must show purchase order numbers and shall be submitted in duplicate to The School Board of Broward County, Florida, Accounts Payable Department, P.O. Box 5408, Fort Lauderdale, Florida 33310-5408. Payment will be made within 30 days after delivery, authorized inspection and acceptance. When vendors are directed to send invoices to a school, the school will make direct payments to the vendor.

26. **NOTE TO VENDORS DELIVERING TO OUR CENTRAL WAREHOUSE:** Receiving hours are Monday through Friday (excluding holidays) **7:00 A.M. to 2:00 P.M.** This warehouse is located on the Seaboard Coast Line siding for rail car routing.

27. **SUBSTITUTIONS:** The School Board of Broward County, Florida *WILL NOT* accept substitute shipments of any kind. Bidder(s) is expected to furnish the brand quoted in their bid once awarded by The School Board. Any substitute shipments will be returned at the bidder's expense.

28. **FACILITIES:** The Board reserves the right to inspect the bidder's facilities at any time with prior notice.

29. **BID ABSTRACTS:** Bidders desiring a copy of bid tabulation may request same by enclosing a self-addressed, stamped envelope with bid.

30. **ASBESTOS STATEMENT:** All material supplied to the School Board of Broward County, Florida must be **100% asbestos free.** Bidder by virtue of bidding, certifies by signing bid, that if awarded any portion of this bid, will supply only material or equipment that is 100% asbestos free. No bid will be considered unless this is agreed to by the vendor.

31. **HOLD HARMLESS AGREEMENT:** During the term of this bid the bidder shall indemnify, hold harmless, and defend the School Board of Broward County, Florida, its agents, servants and employees from any and all costs and expenses, including but not limited to, attorney's fees, reasonable investigative and discovery costs, court costs and all other sums which the Board, its agents, servants and employees may pay or become obligated to pay on account of any, all and every claim or demand, or assertion of liability, or any claim and every claim or demand or assertion of liability, or any claim or actions founded, thereon, arising or alleged to have arisen out of the products, goods or services furnished by the bidder, his agents, servants or employees, or any of his equipment when such persons or equipment are on premises owned or controlled by the Board for the purpose of performing services, delivering products or goods, installing equipment, or otherwise transacting business, whether such claim or claims be for damages, injury to person or property, including the Board's property, or death of any person, group or organization, whether employed by the bidder or the Board or otherwise.

32. The Public Entity Crimes Sworn Statement required under Florida Statutes 287.133(3)a. must be completed and sworn to in the manner prescribed by law and submitted at the time of bid submittal. **Failure to comply with this requirement will result in disqualification of bid submitted.**

BID PROPOSAL

SPECIAL CONDITIONS

1. The School Board of Broward County, Florida, desires bids to **FURNISH & INSTALL NEW LIBRARY SHELVING AND FURNITURE** as specified herein. Prices quoted shall include delivery to **Markham Elementary School, 1501 N. W. 15 Avenue, Pompano Beach, Florida 33060.**

2. **DELIVERY:** Bidder shall indicate, in the space provided on the Bid Summary Sheet, length of delivery time required after receipt of purchase order (ARO). Delivery and installation requirements are expected to be a maximum of ninety (90) days ARO.

3. **AWARD:** Items in groups as marked, shall be awarded **BY GROUP.** Therefore, it is necessary for a bidder to bid on every item in the particular group on which they're submitting a bid in order to have the bid considered. It is also required that the bidder carefully consider each item and make sure that each one meets the specifications as indicated. In the event that one item within a group does not meet such specifications, the entire group bid will be disqualified.

4. **BID REQUIREMENTS:** Bid Security, Performance and Payment Bond and Insurance requirements outlined on attached sheet apply to this bid (copy attached). In addition, full release of lien will be required before final payment is made. Bidder shall take special notice that the **School Board of Broward County, Florida, shall be named as an additional named insured under General Liability Insurance including Contractual Liability. IF BID SECURITY IS A BID BOND, THE ENCLOSED BID BOND FORM MUST BE USED BY THE BIDDERS. NO OTHER BID BOND FORM WILL BE ACCEPTABLE.**

5. **CORRECTION OF WORK:** The successful bidder shall re-execute any work that fails to conform to the requirements of this bid and that appears during the progress of the work and shall remedy any defects due to faulty materials or workmanship which appear within a period of **one (1) year** from the date of completion of installation. Such completion date being considered as the day of final payment.

6. **INSPECTION, ACCEPTANCE & TITLE:** Inspection and acceptance will be at the job site unless otherwise provided. Title to/or risk of loss or damages to all work shall be the responsibility of the successful bidder until accepted by the buyer unless loss or damage results from negligence by the buyer.

7. **SHOP DRAWINGS:** Before award can be made, **and within ten (10) days of request,** apparent low bidder meeting specifications, terms and conditions shall submit with such promptness as to cause no delay to their work, **three (3) copies** of shop drawings for approval. These shop drawings are to be submitted to **Jane Klasing, Director of Learning Resources.**

8. **LEGAL REQUIREMENTS:** Federal, State, County and Local laws, ordinances, rules and regulations that in any manner affect the items covered herein apply. Lack of knowledge by the bidder will in no way be a cause for relief from responsibility.

VENDOR NAME: _____
SS/lc

The School Board of Broward County, Florida
FURNISH & INSTALL SHELVING AND FURNITURE

SPECIAL CONDITIONS (Continued)

9. **WORK SCHEDULE:** The successful bidder shall take the necessary safety precautions to protect personnel and property while the work is in progress, and arrange a work schedule with **Jane Klasing, Director of Learning Resources (305) 765-6154.**

10. **ASBESTOS AND FORMALDEHYDE STATEMENT:** All building materials, pressed boards, and furniture supplied to the School Board of Broward County, Florida, must be **100% asbestos free.** It is desirous that all building materials, pressed boards and furniture supplied to the School Board also be formaldehyde free. Bidder by virtue of bidding certifies by signing bid that is awarded any portion of this bid, will supply only building materials, pressed boards, and/or furniture that is **100% asbestos free.** No bid will be considered unless this is agree to by the vendor.

11. **ITEMIZED LISTING:** For the purpose of inventory information required by the Property and Inventory Department, Bidder must attach to submitted bid a separate, itemized listing of all furniture and shelving offered to Markham Elementary School. Listing shall include quantities of each piece of furniture and shelving required herein and its manufacturer, model number, description, unit price and extended price. **Bids submitted without this information will not be considered for award.**

12. **TERMS AND CONDITIONS:** The School Board of Broward County, Florida, will not accept terms and conditions shown on information submitted with bid. Bidder, by virtue of submitting a bid, agrees to the terms and conditions stated herein.

13. **PLANS:** Detailed plans may be obtained in the Purchasing Department, 1320 Southwest 4th Street, Fort Lauderdale, Florida 33312 **between 8:00 a.m. and 4:00 p.m.**

14. **ALTERNATE BIDS:** Catalog numbers, manufacturers and brand names, when listed, are informational guides as to a standard of acceptable product quality level only and should not be construed as a limitation of manufacturers.

15. **DESCRIPTIVE LITERATURE REQUIREMENTS:** If bidding other than the make(s) and model(s) specified in this Bid, it is required that **COMPLETE DESCRIPTIVE TECHNICAL LITERATURE ON THE ITEM BEING BID, BE SUBMITTED WITH THE BID.** Such literature shall be in sufficient detail to indicate conformance with the specifications of the make(s) and model(s) specified in the bid. **FAILURE TO PROVIDE THIS DESCRIPTIVE LITERATURE IN SUFFICIENT DETAIL TO COMPLETE THE EVALUATION OF THE MAKE(S) AND MODEL(S) OFFERED IN THIS BID, WITH THE BID, WILL RESULT IN DISQUALIFICATION OF BID SUBMITTED.**

16. **GUARANTEE:** All library shelving, furniture and equipment furnished under this contract shall be guaranteed for a period of **one (1) year** against defects in materials and workmanship. If at any time during this period a defect should occur in any item of equipment, that item shall be replaced or repaired by the successful bidder at no obligation on the part of the buyer, except where it shall be shown that the defect is a result of misuse of the furniture and not caused by faulty manufacturing or installation.

VENDOR NAME: _____

The School Board of Broward County, Florida
FURNISH & INSTALL SHELVING AND FURNITURE

SPECIAL CONDITIONS (Continued)

17. **SAMPLE REQUIRED:** Card Catalog Drawer: Each bidder shall supply sample with bid or within **seven (7) calendar days** of written request. Each bidder shall supply sample core of top construction for tables, end panels and shelving tops with bid or within **seven (7) calendar days** of written request.

18. **INSTALLATION REFERENCES:**

Shelving: Each bidder shall cite below the closest location of a recent shelving installation.
NAME AND ADDRESS OF SHELVING INSTALLATION LOCATION:

_____

_____

_____

Wood Furniture: Each bidder shall cite below the closest location of a recent wood furniture installation.

NAME AND ADDRESS OF FURNITURE INSTALLATION LOCATION:

_____

_____

_____

19. **SEALED BID REQUIREMENTS:** The original "Invitation to Bid" sheet must be completed, signed, and returned. In addition, all **Special Condition pages** and only the **Bid Summary pages** on which the bidder actually submits a bid need to be executed and submitted with this bid. **Bids received that fail to comply with these requirements shall not be considered for award.**

20. **SUBMITTAL OF BIDS:** All bidders are reminded that it is the sole responsibility of the **BIDDER** to assure that their bid is **time stamped** in the **PURCHASING DEPARTMENT prior to 2:00 p.m. on date due.** The label attached to the bid solicitation indicates the Post Office address as: P.O. Box 5408, Fort Lauderdale, Florida 33310-5408. The **street address** for hand delivery and **overnight courier** is indicated as: 1320 S.W. 4th Street, Fort Lauderdale, Florida 33312.

21. **POSTING OF BID RECOMMENDATIONS/TABULATIONS:** Bid Recommendations and Tabulations will be posted in the Purchasing Department on _____, and will remain posted for 72 hours. Failure to file a protest **at the office of the Director of Purchasing, 1320 S.W. Fourth Street, Fort Lauderdale, Florida 33312,** within the time prescribed in Section 120.53(5), Florida Statutes, shall constitute a waiver of proceedings under Chapter 120, Florida Statutes. Section 120.53(5)(b), Florida Statutes, states that **"The formal written protest shall state with particularity the facts and law upon which the protest is based".**

VENDOR NAME: _____

The School Board of Broward County, Florida
FURNISH & INSTALL SHELVING AND FURNITURE

SPECIAL CONDITIONS (Continued)

22. **INFORMATION:** Any questions by prospective bidders concerning this Invitation to Bid should be addressed to _____, **Purchasing Agent, Purchasing Department, (305) 765-6086** who is authorized only to direct the attention of prospective bidders to various portions of the Bid so they may read and interpret such for themselves. Neither _____ nor any employee of the School Board of Broward County is authorized to interpret any portion of the Bid or give information as to the requirements of the Bid in addition to that contained in the written Bid Document. Interpretations of the Bid or additional information as to its requirements, where necessary, shall be communicated to bidders only by written addendum.

BID SUMMARY SHEET

TOTAL COST

<u>ITEM 1:</u>   **(TO BE AWARDED AS A GROUP)**

A.   Furnish and install metal shelving and wood furniture as per specifications and plans at:

Markham Elementary School $_____
1501 N. W. 15 Avenue
Pompano Beach, FL 33060

Installation is to include furnishing all necessary materials, equipment, machinery, tools, apparatus, means of transportation and labor to complete this project.

Delivery & Installation: _____ days ARO

NOTE: Bidder shall attach to Bid submitted an itemized listing of the metal shelving and wood furniture to be installed for Bid Item 1A, as per Special Condition 11.

VENDOR NAME: _____

The School Board of Broward County, Florida
FURNISH & INSTALL SHELVING AND FURNITURE

BID SPECIFICATIONS

LIBRARY SHELVING AND FURNITURE

I. **SCOPE:**

    A.   It is the intent of this bid to purchase and have installed quality and functional shelving and furniture at Markham Elementary school. Wood furniture shall have solid lumber core for all table tops and carrels. A study has been made of specific minimum standards acceptable for these items in order to function properly, and it is these minimum standards that constitute this specification. Sample core of top construction may be requested within seven (7) calendar days of written request to individual vendors.

    B.   The shelving and furniture as illustrated and as specified herein shall be delivered to the buildings in pre-finished units. Shelving/furniture shall be set in place, leveled, secured to walls or floors where necessary and trimmed or scribed to make a COMPLETE INSTALLATION OF HIGHEST QUALITY.

    C.   The successful bidder shall furnish all accessory equipment, hardware and miscellaneous materials as specified herein.

    D.   The successful bidder shall provide and be responsible for all cutouts in shelving/furniture as required for all electrical and mechanical connections.

    E.   The successful bidder shall keep the premises free from accumulation of waste material and rubbish and, at completion of the work, they shall remove from the premises all rubbish, implements, and surplus materials and leave the building broom clean.

II. **STEEL SHELVING:**

    A.   **SCOPE OF WORK:** This specification covers delivery and installation of library shelving of the bracket type only in accordance with these specifications and plans. Unit heights, depths and accessories shall be as indicated on the plans and/or schedule of equipment. All shelving shall be carefully adjusted to the floor and leveled. Wall shelving shall be attached to the walls at the most inconspicuous locations.

    B.   **MATERIALS AND WORKMANSHIP:** Only the finest materials and quality of workmanship will be acceptable. Commercial grade or case-type shelving will not be considered. Sheet metal is to be furniture stock, cold rolled, reannealed and full pickled or equivalent. Gauge thickness are U.S. standard with the following minimum requirements.

        1.   Upright columns of welded frame or sway brace construction, #16 gauge.

VENDOR NAME: _____

The School Board of Broward County, Florida
FURNISH & INSTALL SHELVING AND FURNITURE

BID SPECIFICATIONS (Continued)

LIBRARY SHELVING AND FURNITURE

II.   **STEEL SHELVING (Continued):**

B.   **MATERIALS AND WORKMANSHIP (Continued):**

2.   Top and bottom spreaders of welded frame or sway brace construction #16 gauge.

3.   Shelves (including base shelf) #18 gauge.

4.   Shelf end brackets, #16 gauge.

C.   **CAPACITY REQUIREMENTS:** Each shelf shall have a minimum clearance between end brackets of 35-7/16".

D.   **FINISH:** Component parts shall be prepared for painting by a multistage cleaning and phosphatizing process. Material is then to be finished with fine baking enamel of medium gloss, applied by electrostatic method, capable of withstanding severe hammer and bending tests without flaking. Surfaces difficult to cover electrostatically are to be hand sprayed prior to entering baking ovens, allowing uniform and complete paint coverage. Coverage shall be capable of withstanding a minimum of 200 hours in a spray chamber (per ASTM Method No. B117) as well as all normal resistances of a quality finish.

E.   **COLOR:** Manufacturer's standard colors to be selected.

F.   **TYPE OF BOOKSTACK:** Steel bookstacks are to be of unit construction using welded frame or sway-brace with starter, adder configuration, such that all components of a bookstack section may be removed from any range without in any way disturbing the adjacent units. There are to be no exposed welds, or that all exposed welds to be polished clean.

1.   Upright columns of welded frames or sway-brace construction shall be formed of not less than #16 gauge steel into channel shape with no less than 1/2" stiffening flanges measuring 2" in the web and 1-1/2" at front and rear surfaces. Uprights are to be perforated full height with a series of 3/16" × 5/8" slots spaced 1" on vertical centers and located within 5/16" from the web. Every fifth and sixth slot shall be spaced differently to ease visual leveling of adjustable shelves. Top spreader of welded frames or sway-brace construction will consist of not less than #16 gauge tubular steel shape measuring at least 1" × 2-1/2" on cross section.

VENDOR NAME: _____

The School Board of Broward County, Florida
FURNISH & INSTALL SHELVING AND FURNITURE

BID SPECIFICATIONS (Continued)

LIBRARY SHELVING AND FURNITURE

II. **STEEL SHELVING (Continued):**

F. **TYPE OF BOOKSTACK (Continued):**

1. (Continued)

   Bottom spreader of welded frame or sway-brace construction will consist of not less than #16 gauge steel channel shaped measuring at least 1" × 1-3/4" in cross section. The outer ends of this channel are to be punched and will receive weld nuts pre-drilled to receive floor leveler guides. Welded frames or sway-brace construction shall be of heights as specified, and 36" wide or of special widths as specified and equipped with two (2) adjustable neoprene covered glides to provide protection to floor covering and to prevent "walking" of stack units.

2. Closed base support brackets shall be designed to fit snugly in and around uprights. Material shall be no less than #16 gauge steel. Brackets shall have a 90 degree flange at bottom which will rest on floor covering. Capability to level bookstack unit shall be incorporated into the base bracket. Top and front edge of base bracket shall match that of adjustable shelves end bracket and in addition shall have a hole in the impression for attaching adjoining base brackets with fasteners contained within the impression.

3. Closed base shelves shall be formed of not less than #18 gauge steel into one piece construction designed to fit snugly around upright columns and base brackets without need of hardware fasteners. Front height shall be approximately 3" and sides shall have stiffening flanges.

4. Adjustable shelves shall be formed of no less than #18 gauge steel with front and rear edges box formed 3/4" high, capable of receiving wire book supports and snap-on label holders. Nominal depths of shelf shall be 1" greater than actual dimension measured from front of shelf to frame upright. Side of shelves to be flanged for locking into end bracket grip. Shelves shall support book loads of 40 pounds per square foot without deflecting in excess of 3/16".

5. Shelf end brackets designed with a 15 degree sloped front edge shall be formed of not less than #16 gauge steel and all but the rear edge is to be flanged outward approximately 1/4". Rear edge shall have two (2) crimped hooks at top and a positioning tab at bottom for engaging frame upright slots. Incorporate two (2) grips for securing shelf side flanges; also include cup impression to prevent bracket overlapment when units are shelved. Brackets shall extend at least 6" above shelf surface.

VENDOR NAME: _____

The School Board of Broward County, Florida
FURNISH & INSTALL SHELVING AND FURNITURE

BID SPECIFICATIONS (Continued)

LIBRARY SHELVING AND FURNITURE

II. **STEEL SHELVING (Continued):**

    F. **TYPE OF BOOKSTACK (Continued):**

        6.

HEIGHT	ADJUSTABLE SHELVES
66"	4
42"	2

        7. Divider type shelf shall be of no less than #18 gauge steel with front edge box formed 3/4" high and with back edge formed upward 5" and with 1/4" return, shelf to be slotted on 1" centers to receive divided plates, include five (5) divider plates 6" high for each shelf opening unless other quantities or heights are specified. Divider shelves are to be of actual depth as specified.

        8. Magazine shelving shall be of similar construction to other shelving. It shall be 12" deep with fixed slope for display. The units shall be single faced, 66" high having four (4) sloped shelves when shown as wall mounted shelving or 42" high having three (3) sloped shelves when shown as free standing.

        9. High pressure laminate (.050 w/.050 backing; simultaneously applied) on all 42" and lower shelving end panels, provide continuous tops 1-1/4" thick, with high pressure laminate as selected on top and edges over 45 pound density particle board cores. Provide matching laminate on underside. Fillers shall be of identical laminate over 45 pound density particle board cores. Support with #12 gauge brackets.

        10. Finished end panels shall be of high pressure laminate, color to be selected, minimum 3/4" thickness. End panels shall be on all shelving where appropriate. All starter and final sections of ranges will have end panels whether free standing, wall mounted, or perpendicular to walls. Filler sections shall be used where appropriate. No final sections shall end without end panel or filler.

        11. Finished tops shall be of high pressure laminate as in II F.9. Tops shall be on all shelving 42" and lower.

    G. **ACCESSORIES:**

        1. Book supports/findable plate-type book supports 6" high shall be of #16 gauge steel, designed to match shelf and bracket profile and to include non-skid composition on base. Paint to match shelving color. Provide one for each base shelf and for all adjustable shelves.

VENDOR NAME: _____

The School Board of Broward County, Florida
FURNISH & INSTALL SHELVING AND FURNITURE

BID SPECIFICATIONS (Continued)

LIBRARY SHELVING AND FURNITURE

II. **STEEL SHELVING (Continued):**

G. **ACCESSORIES (Continued):**

2. Shelf backstops shall be of #20 gauge steel, 3″ high with return stiffening flanges and hooks for engaging upright column slots. Backstops are to be self-hanging and independent of shelves and/or brackets, so that shelves can be raised or lowered without disturbing backstop. Backstops shall be furnished for all freestanding double faced areas.

3. Four (4) stack hanging carrels (35-7/8″ W × 24″ D) with leg supports and high pressure laminate work surfaces as per II F.9 to be located in shelving at discretion of schools' library media staff.

H. **COLORS:** Color of steel shelving and laminate to be selected.

III. **WOOD FURNITURE FOR MARKHAM ELEMENTARY SCHOOL:**

A. **MODULAR CHARGING DESK:** Shall be 30″ to 32″ standing height for elementary schools, include individual tops for each module, and include the following:

QUANTITY	DESCRIPTION	BUCKSTAFF #	LIBRARY BUREAU #	BRODART #
1	Discharge Unit	6806-307	90-0-7400	60-166
2	Corner Units	6811-118	90-0-7410	60-150
1	Knee Space Unit	6807-308	90-0-7402	60-175
1	Book Return Unit	6813-315	90-0-7408	60-167
1	Depressible Book Truck	6427-000	90-0-7660.15D	60-915
2	End Panels	6800-000	7415	60-178
1	**Printer Stand**		**7400 MPS**	
* 1	**Computer Circulation Unit, (as per the following specifications):**		**7422RTCCU**	

Computer Circulation Unit, intermembering; Minimum 67″ L × 26-3/4″ D × 30″ H with Tambor roll lockable top for security which rises in groove of shroud, which rises a minimum of 17-1/2″ above desk work surface, including wire management channel positioned below work surface with lockable, hinged, vertical wood chase (rear corner) providing wire management system to floor on one side, drawer pedestal opposite side, mobile printer stand with one base shelf, one adjustable paper storage shelf, rear paper feed slot, hidden paper storage.

    Above model numbers or equivalent.
* The **Computer Circulation Unit** shall be as described in the specifications shown and shall be equivalent in construction to the other listed components of the modular charging desk.

VENDOR NAME: _____

The School Board of Broward County, Florida
FURNISH & INSTALL SHELVING AND FURNITURE

BID SPECIFICATIONS (Continued)

LIBRARY SHELVING AND FURNITURE

III. **WOOD FURNITURE FOR MARKHAM ELEMENTARY SCHOOL (Continued):**

B. **CARD CATALOGS:**

QUANTITY	DESCRIPTION	BUCKSTAFF #	LIBRARY BUREAU #	BRODART #
5	Top	6831-218	90W-T	60-886
5	15 Drawer Unit *	6431-502	93515R	60-890
5	16" Leg Base	6831-203	90W-16B	60-891

* Trays with wooden fronts and plastic tray bodies.

Above model numbers or equivalent.

C. **DICTIONARY STANDS:**

QUANTITY	DESCRIPTION	BUCKSTAFF #	LIBRARY BUREAU #	BRODART #
1	Dictionary Stand	6835-194	90W-DS	60-869

D. **FURNITURE:**

QUANTITY	DESCRIPTION	BUCKSTAFF #	LIBRARY BUREAU #	BRODART #
66	Chairs-16" depth, 30" overall height, wood seat & back	6889-301	76S	A1-561
6	Tables-w/wood base, rectangle 36" × 60", 27-1/2" high	6859-136	90W-3660	64-144
6	Round table, 48" w/wood legs, 27-1/2" high	6859-167	90W-48	64-141

Informal furniture-upholstery
color to be selected

VENDOR NAME: _____

The School Board of Broward County, Florida
FURNISH & INSTALL SHELVING AND FURNITURE

BID SPECIFICATIONS (Continued)

LIBRARY SHELVING AND FURNITURE

III. **WOOD FURNITURE FOR MARKHAM ELEMENTARY SCHOOL (Continued):**

 D. **FURNITURE (Continued):**

QUANTITY	DESCRIPTION	BUCKSTAFF #	LIBRARY BUREAU #	BRODART #
1	3-Seat lounge	6892-123	8113-3	L1-302
3	Chairs	6892-111	8113-1	L1-102
1	Sloped top table, wood base	6854-194	SL90W	64-142
2	Bench wood base	6855-194	B90W-14	64-147
1	Horizontal exhibit case		82W-9771	64-450

 E. **BOOKTRUCKS:**

QUANTITY	DESCRIPTION	BUCKSTAFF #	LIBRARY BUREAU #	BRODART #
3	Mobile display book trucks, 2 sloping shelves, 4 swivel casters	6425-240	7609	60919

 F. **COLOR:** Color and finish to be selected.

VENDOR NAME: _____

BID BOND

STATE OF FLORIDA   )

COUNTY OF BROWARD   )

    KNOW ALL MEN BY THESE PRESENTS, that we, _____

_____ (hereinafter called "Principal") and

_____, a corporation chartered

and doing business under the laws of the State of _____ and authorized

under the laws of the State of Florida and approved by the U.S. Treasury Department to act as surety

on bonds, as "Surety" (hereinafter called "Surety") are held and firmly bound unto the School

Board of Broward County, Florida, a body corporate (hereinafter called the "Owner"),

in the sum of _____

_____ Dollars ($_____) lawful money of the United States

of America, to be paid to the School Board of Broward County, Florida, for which payment well and

truly made, we bind ourselves, our successors, and several respective heirs, executors, administrators,

and assigns, jointly and severally, firmly by these presents:

    WHEREAS, the above bounden "Principal" contemplates submitting or has submitted a

proposal to the said "Owner" for furnishing all necessary labor, materials, equipment,

machinery, tools, apparatus, and means of transportation for the construction of: _____

_____, and,

    WHEREAS, it was a condition precedent to the submission of said bid that a certified check or

bid bond in the amount of five percent (5%) of the base bid be submitted with said bid as a guarantee

that the bidder would, if awarded the contract, enter into a written contract with the said The School

Board of Broward County and furnish a contract surety bond, issued by a surety company approved by

the U.S. Treasury Department, licensed to do business in Florida, and executed and signed by a resident

agent having an office in Florida, representing such Surety company, in an amount equal to one

hundred percent (100%) of the Contract price for the performance of said contract within fifteen (15)

consecutive calendar days after written notice having been given of the Contract.

    NOW, THEREFORE, THE CONDITIONS OF THIS OBLIGATION ARE SUCH, that if the proposal

of the "Principal" herein be accepted and said "Principal" within fifteen (15) consecutive calendar days

after written notice being given of such acceptance, enter into a written contract with the said

"Owner" and furnish a contract Surety bond in an amount equal to one hundred percent (100%) of the

contract price, satisfactory to the said "Owner", then this obligation shall be void; otherwise, the sum herein stated shall be due and payable to The School Board of Broward County, Florida, and the "Surety" herein agrees to pay said sum immediately upon demand of said School Board of Broward County, in good and lawful money of the United States of America, as liquidated damages for failure thereof of the said "Principal."

IN WITNESS WHEREOF, the said _____ as "Principal" herein, has caused these presents to be signed in its name by its

_____, and attested by its _____

under its corporate seal, and the said _____

as "Surety" herein, has caused these presents to be signed in its name by its

_____, and attested by its _____

under its corporate seal this _____ day of _____, A.D.,

19_____ .

_____

BY _____
　　　　　　　　　　　　　　　　Title

_____

BY _____
　　　　　　　　　　　　　　　　Title

ATTEST:

_____

TITLE _____

_____

TITLE _____

SPECIAL CONDITION REQUIREMENTS

1. **BID SECURITY:** A Surety Bond, Certified Check, Cashier's Check, Treasurer's Check or bank draft of any State or National Bank representing 5% of the total amount of the bid must accompany bid. Bonding company must appear on U.S. Treasury list.

2. **PERFORMANCE AND PAYMENT BOND:** The successful bidder shall furnish a surety bond as security for faithful performance of orders(s) awarded as a result of this bid, and for the payment of all persons performing labor, and on their furnishing materials in connection therewith. Surety of such bond shall be in an amount equal to the bid. The Attorney-in-Fact who signs the bond must file with the bond a certificate and effective dated copy of power of attorney. Bonding company must appear on U.S. Treasury list. Performance and payment bond must be forwarded to the Director of Internal Services within fifteen (15) days of notification of award of this contract. If this bond is not received said bid will be subject to cancellation.

3. **REQUEST FOR PAYMENT** whether partial or final, in excess of $500.00 must be accompanied by a "Full or Partial Release of Lien". The successful bidder will receive a blank copy of the release with the purchase order. Additional copies of the release may be obtained from the office of the Director of Internal Services.

4. **INSURANCE REQUIREMENTS:**
Proof of the following insurance will be furnished by the successful bidder to the Board by Certificate of Insurance. Such certificate must contain a provision for notification of the Board 30 days in advance of any material change in coverage or cancellation.

1. General Liability Insurance, including Contractual Liability to cover the "Hold Harmless Agreement" set forth herein, with bodily injury limits of not less than $300,000 per occurrence combined single limit bodily injury and property damage. The School Board of Broward County, Florida shall be named as an additional insured.

2. Product Liability or Completed Operations Insurance with bodily injury limits of liability of not less than $300,000 per occurrence and $300,000 aggregate.

3. Auto Liability Insurance with bodily injury limits of not less than $100,000 per person; $300,000 per occurrence and property damage limits of not less than $50,000.

4. Worker's Compensation and Employer's Liability Insurance with a limit of not less than $100,000 per occurrence.

The successful bidder agrees, by accepting the award of this bid, to the following "Hold Harmless Agreement".

During the term of this bid the vendor shall indemnify, hold harmless, and defend the School Board of Broward County, Florida, its agents, servants and employees from any and all costs and expenses, including but not limited to, attorney's fees, reasonable investigative and discovery costs, court costs and all other sums which the Board, its agents, servants and employees may pay or become obligated to pay on account of any, all and every claim or demand, or assertion of liability, or any claim and every claim or demand or assertion of liability, or any claim or action founded, thereon, arising or alleged to have arisen out of the products, goods or services furnished by the vendor, his agents, servants or employees, or any of his equipment when such persons or equipment are on premises owned or controlled by the Board for the purpose of performing services, delivering products or goods, installing equipment, or otherwise transacting business, whether such claim or claims be for damages, injury to person or property, including the Board's property, or death of any person, group or organization, whether employed by the vendor or the Board or otherwise.

Any questions as to the intent or meaning of any part of the above required coverages should be brought to the Director of Risk Management of the School Board of Broward County, Florida.

SCHOOL BOARD OF BROWARD COUNTY FLORIDA
Learning Resources Department

BID ANALYSIS

	1st Low Bid	2nd Low Bid	3rd Low Bid	4th Low Bid
Special Conditions:				
Packaged Bid				
Itemized Listing				
Descriptive Literature				
Bid Security				
Shelving:				
Uprights (#16 gauge)				
Spreaders Top (#16 gauge)				
Spreaders Bottom (#16 gauge)				
Closed Base Support Brackets (#16 gauge)				
Closed Base Shelves (#16 gauge)				
Shelves (#18 gauge)				
Shelf End (#16 gauge)				
Clearance (35 7/16″ min) between end brackets (width)				
Finish				
Baked Enamel				
Electrostatic				
Frame				
Welded or /Sway Brace				
Starter-Adder Configuration				
Uprights - Perforation				
Full Height				
3/16″ × 5/8″ Slots				
1″ Spacing (vertical centers)				

BID ANALYSIS

	1st Low Bid	2nd Low Bid	3rd Low Bid	4th Low Bid
Shelves:				
Adjustable				
Edges 3/4" h				
Snap-on Label Holders				
Wire Book Support Channel				
Sides Flanged				
Support 40 lbs/p/sq. ft.				
Laminate:				
Continuous Tops				
1 1/4" Thick Tops				
High pressure .050 w/ .050 backing				
45 lb. Density Particle Board				
3/4" Thick End Panels				
Accessories:				
Booksupports				
6" h				
#16 gauge				
Nonskid Base				
Backstops				
#20 gauge/3" high				
Self Hanging				
Picture Book Dividers				
Hanging Stack Carrels				
35" x 24"				
Leg Supports				

BID ANALYSIS

	1st Low Bid	2nd Low Bid	3rd Low Bid	4th Low Bid
Modular Charging Desk:				
_____ " h				
Units:				
Discharge				
Corner				
Knee Space				
Book return				
Depressible Book Truck				
End Panels				
Computer Circulation				
Typing Desk Unit				
Card Catalogs:				
_____ Tops				
_____ Drawer Units				
_____ Base				
Dictionary Stand				
Furniture:				
_____ Chairs				
_____ Tables - Rectangular				
_____ Tables - Round				
Sloped Topped Table (wood base)				
Bench (wood base)				
3 Seat Lounge				
Chairs				
Book Trucks				
Horizontal Exhibit Case				

APPENDIX E

General Information
on
Shelving and Layouts

A. Shelving section width—3 feet

B. Heights of shelving

   (1) 42″ & 60″ for Elementary Schools

   (2) 60″ & 82″ for Junior High (Middle) Schools

   (3) 60″ & 82″ for Senior High Schools

   (4) 42″ counter shelving (freestanding, island type, 6″-9″h upright dividers for picture books)

C. Depth of shelves

   (1) 10″ standard

   (2) 12″ & 16″ oversize and picture books

   (3) 12″ magazines

   (4) 16″ audiovisual materials

D. All shelving adjustable

   (1) 42″ High Single Face—3 adjustable shelves per unit, 90 volumes per section.

   (2) 60″ High Single Face—5 adjustable shelves per unit, 150 volumes per section.

   (3) 82″ High Single Face—6 adjustable shelves per unit, 210 volumes per section.

   (4) 96″ High Single Face—7 adjustable shelves per unit, 240 volumes per section.

E. Capacity estimates

   Books per shelf

   30 average size

   60 picture books

   15-18 reference books

F. *Seating Capacity* should be 10% to 15% of the total school enrollment.

   Book Capacity should be 100 times the seating capacity.

   Magazine Capacity should be 50% to 75% of the library seating capacity. Three magazines per shelf can be displayed.

   Book Stacks should be positioned for adequate supervision from the charge desk. 3′ space should be allowed between stacks.

APPENDIX F

Furniture and Shelving Templates

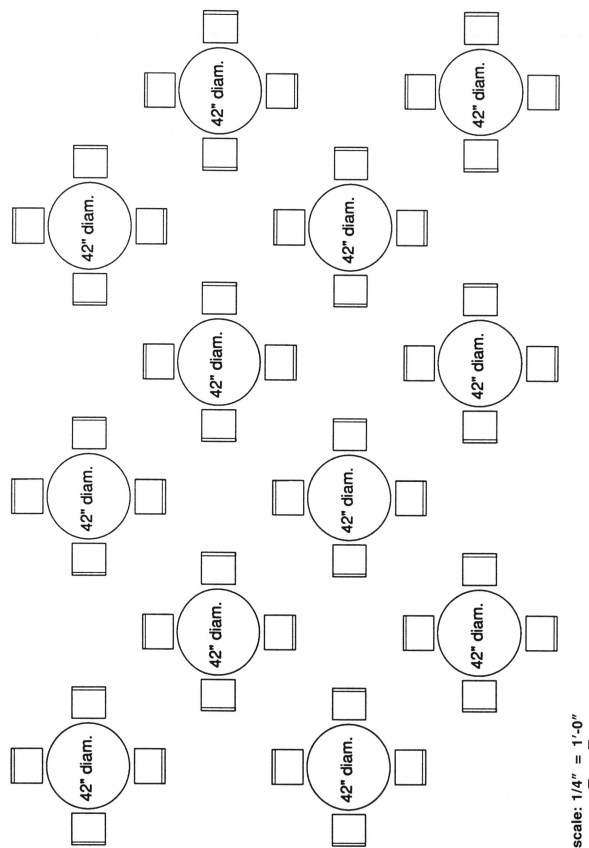

scale: 1/4" = 1'-0"

tables

allow 4' clear between tables and 5' clear at shelving units

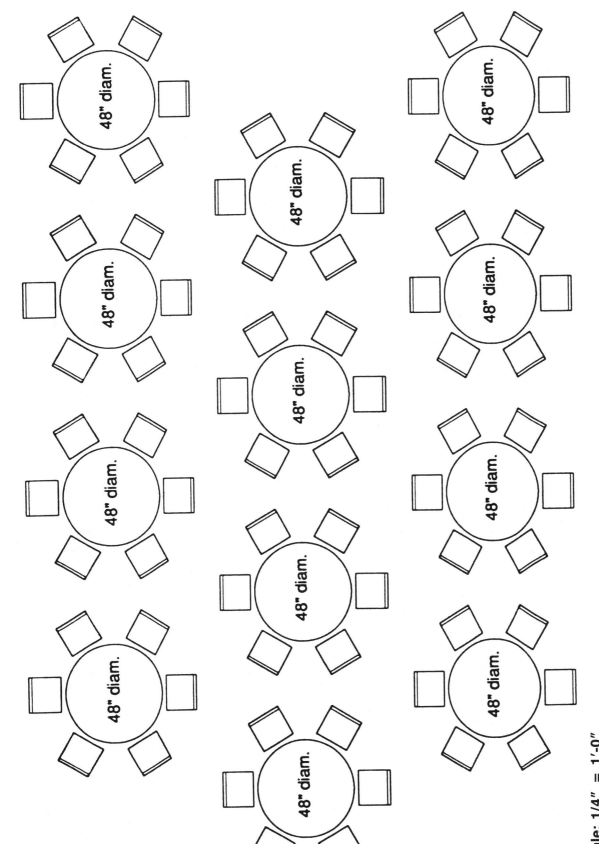

48" diam.

scale: 1/4" = 1'-0"

tables

allow 4' clear between tables and 5' clear at shelving units

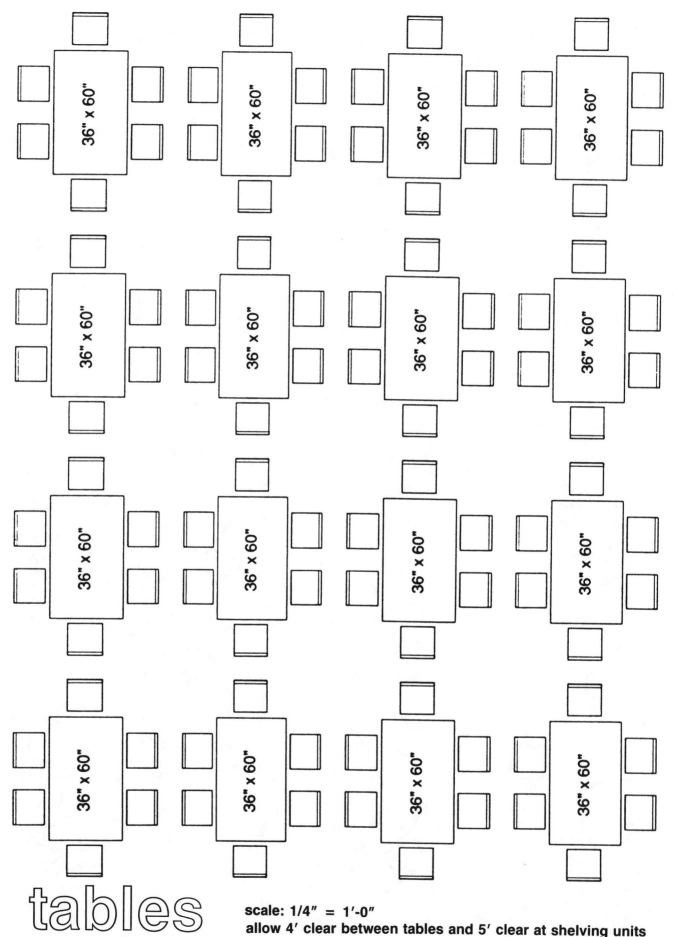

tables

scale: 1/4" = 1'-0"
allow 4' clear between tables and 5' clear at shelving units

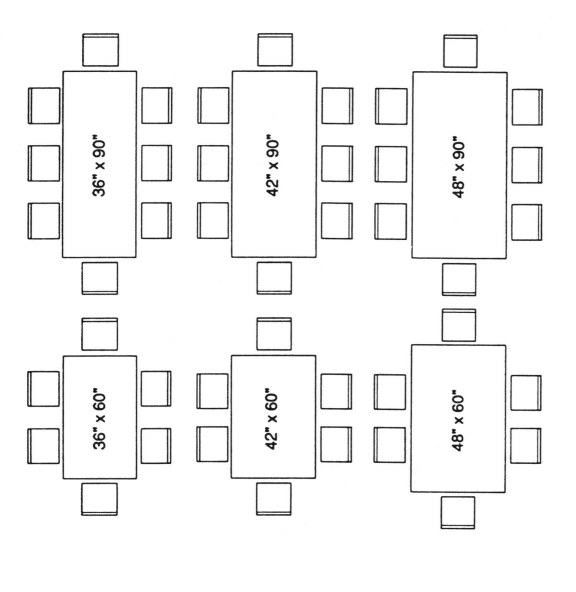

10" shelves | 10" shelves | 10" shelves | 10" shelves | 10" shelves | 10" shelves

36" x 90"

42" x 90"

48" x 90"

36" x 60"

42" x 60"

48" x 60"

scale: 1/4" = 1'-0"
allow 4' clear between tables and 5' clear at shelving units

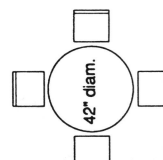

42" diam.

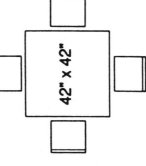

42" x 42"

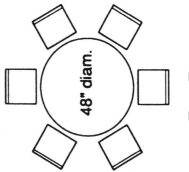

48" diam.

tables

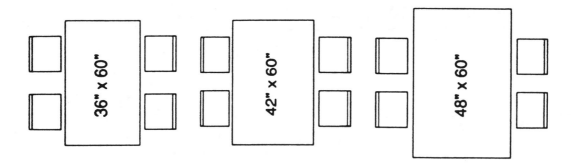

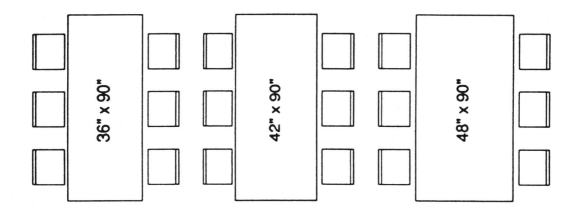

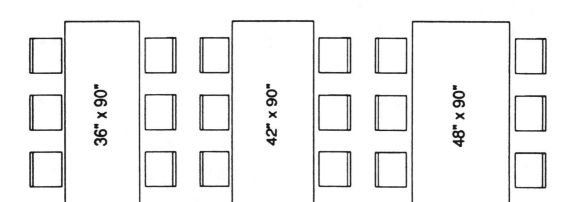

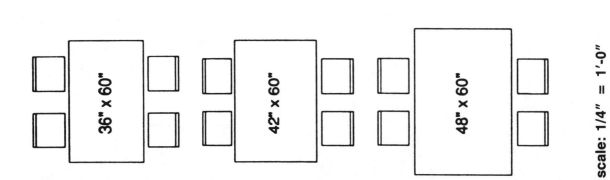

36" x 60"   42" x 60"   48" x 60"

36" x 90"   42" x 90"   48" x 90"

36" x 90"   42" x 90"   48" x 90"

36" x 60"   42" x 60"   48" x 60"

scale: 1/4" = 1'-0"

tables

allow 4' clear between tables and 5' clear at shelving units

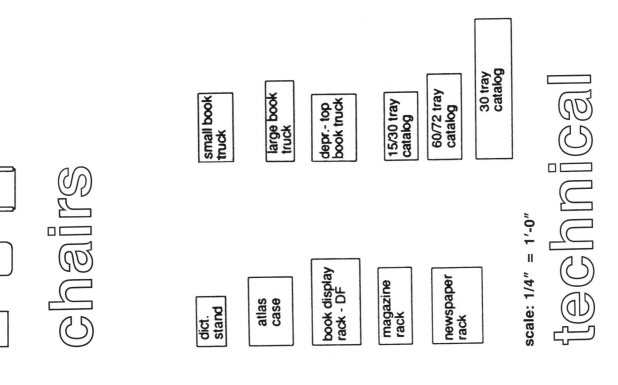

chairs

small book truck

large book truck

depr. - top book truck

15/30 tray catalog

60/72 tray catalog

30 tray catalog

dict. stand

atlas case

book display rack - DF

magazine rack

newspaper rack

scale: 1/4" = 1'-0"

technical

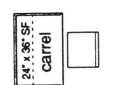

files

2 drawer lateral file

4 drawer lateral file

2 dr. vert. file

4 dr. vert. file

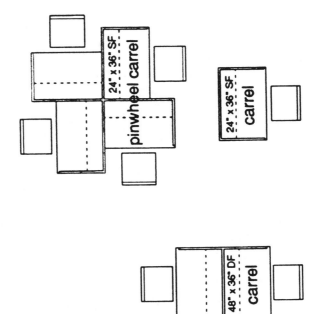

24" x 36" SF carrel

pinwheel carrel

24" x 36" SF

24" x 36" SF carrel

48" x 36" DF carrel

scale: 1/4" = 1'-0"

carrels

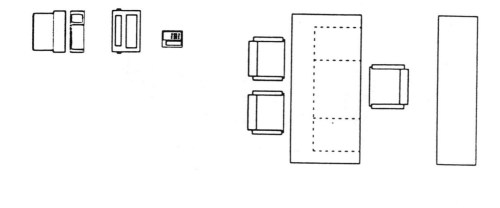

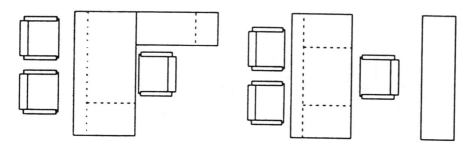

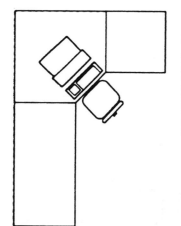

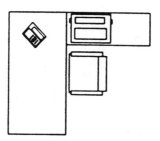

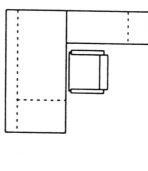

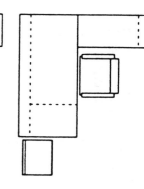

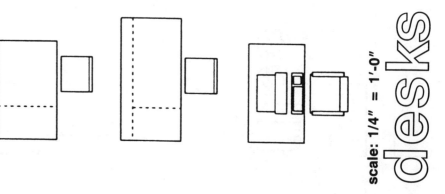

10" shelves	10" shelves	10" shelves	10" shelves	10" shelves	10" shelves	10" shelves	10" shelves	10" shelves	10" shelves	10" shelves	10" shelves
DF 10" shelves	DF 10" shelves	DF 10" shelves	DF 10" shelves	DF 10" shelves	DF 10" shelves	DF 10" shelves	DF 10" shelves	DF 10" shelves	DF 10" shelves	DF 10" shelves	DF 10" shelves
10" shelves	10" shelves	10" shelves	10" shelves	10" shelves	10" shelves	10" shelves	10" shelves	10" shelves	10" shelves	10" shelves	10" shelves
DF 10" shelves	DF 10" shelves	DF 10" shelves	DF 10" shelves	DF 10" shelves	DF 10" shelves	DF 10" shelves	DF 10" shelves	DF 10" shelves	DF 10" shelves	DF 10" shelves	DF 10" shelves
10" shelves	10" shelves	10" shelves	10" shelves	10" shelves	10" shelves	10" shelves	10" shelves	10" shelves	10" shelves	10" shelves	10" shelves
DF 12" shelves	DF 12" shelves	DF 12" shelves	DF 12" shelves	DF 12" shelves	DF 12" shelves	DF 12" shelves	DF 12" shelves	DF 12" shelves	DF 12" shelves	DF 12" shelves	DF 12" shelves
12" shelves	12" shelves	12" shelves	12" shelves	12" shelves	12" shelves	12" shelves	12" shelves	12" shelves	12" shelves	12" shelves	12" shelves
DF 12" shelves	DF 12" shelves	DF 12" shelves	DF 12" shelves	DF 12" shelves	DF 12" shelves	DF 12" shelves	DF 12" shelves	DF 12" shelves	DF 12" shelves	DF 12" shelves	DF 12" shelves
12" shelves	12" shelves	12" shelves	12" shelves	12" shelves	12" shelves	12" shelves	12" shelves	12" shelves	12" shelves	12" shelves	12" shelves
DF 12" shelves	DF 12" shelves	DF 12" shelves	DF 12" shelves	DF 12" shelves	DF 12" shelves	DF 12" shelves	DF 12" shelves	DF 12" shelves	DF 12" shelves	DF 12" shelves	DF 12" shelves
12" shelves	12" shelves	12" shelves	12" shelves	12" shelves	12" shelves	12" shelves	12" shelves	12" shelves	12" shelves	12" shelves	12" shelves

shelves

template layout

scale: 1/4" = 1'-0"

scale: 1/8" = 1'-0"

APPENDIX G

State Publications
on
School Library Media Facilities

This list of publications was compiled from responses to requests sent to each state department of education in 1989. The purpose was to identify any state documents that provide guidelines or facilities requirements. Responses were received from 36 states; several indicated that the documents are in the process of being revised or replaced. Each school to be renovated or newly constructed will have a school planning team that must examine the current state guidelines as part of the planning process.

State Document

Alabama *Space Requirements—Media Center/Library.* Montgomery: Alabama Department of Education, n.d.

Arkansas *Guidelines for Planning School Facilities.* Little Rock: Arkansas Department of Education, 1975.

California *An Instrument for the Qualitative Evaluation of Media Programs in California.* Sacramento: California State Department of Education, 1972.

Colorado *Colorado Information Power: Guidelines for School Library Media Programs.* Denver: Colorado State Board of Education, 1989.

Connecticut *Guide to School Library Media Programs.* Hartford: State of Connecticut, 1982.

Delaware *Media Programs for Delaware Schools: Guidelines for Excellence.* Dover: Delaware Department of Public Instruction, 1975.

Florida *Florida School Library Media Programs: A Guide for Excellence.* Tallahassee: Florida Department of Education.

Hawaii (Document in Progress, Hawaii Department of Education.)

Idaho *Managing School Libraries in Elementary and Secondary Schools.* Boise: Idaho Department of Education, 1986.

Illinois *Recommended Standards for Educational Media Programs in Illinois.* Springfield: Illinois Board of Education, 1986.

Indiana *Guidelines for Indiana School Media Programs.* Indianapolis: Indiana Department of Public Instruction, 1978.

Iowa *Plan for Progress . . . in the Media Center: Facilities.* Des Moines: Iowa Department of Public Instruction, 1973.

Kansas *Guidelines for School Library Media Programs in Kansas.* Topeka: Kansas Association of School Librarians, n.d.

Kentucky *Guidelines for Merit Media Programs.* Frankfort: Kentucky Department of Education, 1985.

Louisiana *Standards and Guidelines for Library Media Programs in Louisiana Schools.* Baton Rouge: Louisiana Department of Education, 1978.

Maine *Media Programs: Guidelines for Maine Schools.* Augusta: Maine Department of Educational and Cultural Services, 1988.

Maryland *Media Center Facility Design for Maryland Schools.* Baltimore: Maryland State Department of Education, 1975.

Michigan *Guidelines for Media Programs in Michigan Schools.* Lansing: Michigan Department of Education, 1979.

Missouri *Learning Resources: A Guide for Learning Resources Programs and Services.* Jefferson City: Missouri State Department of Education, 1975.

New Hampshire *Planning School Library Media Facilities for New Hampshire and Vermont.* Concord: New Hampshire State Department of Education and Vermont Department of Education, 1989.

New Jersey *New Jersey Blueprint for School Media Programs.* Trenton: State of New Jersey, 1979. (New edition in progress.)

New York *Facilities for School Library Media Programs.* Albany: University of the State of New York, State Education Department, 1971.

North Carolina *Media Program Recommendations: Guidelines for School Media Programs at the Individual School and Administrative Unit Levels.* Raleigh: North Carolina Division of Educational Media, 1981.

North Dakota *Handbook for Media Centers in North Dakota Schools.* Bismarck: North Dakota Department of Public Instruction, 1975.

Ohio *A Self-Appraisal Checklist for Library/Media Programs in Ohio (K–12).* Columbus: Ohio Department of Education, 1982.

Oklahoma *Guidelines for Library Media Programs in Oklahoma.* Oklahoma City: Oklahoma State Department of Education, 1985.

Pennsylvania *Pennsylvania Guidelines for School Library Media Programs.* Harrisburg: Pennsylvania Department of Education, 1989.

South Carolina *South Carolina School Facilities Planning and Construction Guide.* Columbia: South Carolina Department of Education.

South Dakota *Planning Guide for School Library Media Programs: A Resource Guide for South Dakota Schools.* Pierre: South Dakota Department of Education and Cultural Affairs, 1985.

Tennessee *Library Media Handbook.* Nashville: Tennessee Department of Education, 1986.

Texas *Library Learning Resources Facilities: New and Remodeled.* Austin: Texas Education Agency, 1982.

Utah *Media: Facilities, Equipment, and Materials.* Salt Lake City: Utah State Board of Education, n.d.

Vermont *Planning School Library Media Facilities for New Hampshire and Vermont.* Concord: New Hampshire State Department of Education and Vermont Department of Education, 1989.

Washington *Standards and Guidelines for Learning Resources.* Olympia: Washington Superintendent of Public Instruction, 1981.

West Virginia *Handbook on Planning School Facilities.* Charleston: West Virginia Department of Education, 1987.

Wyoming *Guidelines for Wyoming School Library Facilities.* Cheyenne: Wyoming State Department of Education, 1983.

INDEX

prepared by M.J. Anderson

Numbers in italic indicate tables, diagrams, graphs, or drawings.